THINK ON THIS

THINK ON THIS

Truths of Life

James W. Bryant

XULON PRESS

Liberty Hill Press
2301 Lucien Way #415
Maitland, FL 32751
407.339.4217
www.libertyhillpublishing.com

Unless otherwise indicated, Scripture quotations taken from the King James Version (KJV) – *public domain.*

Printed in the United States of America.

Paperback ISBN-13: 978-1-6628-0164-8
Dust Jacket ISBN-13: 978-1-6628-0165-5
Ebook ISBN-13: 978-1-6628-0166-2

Foreword

Think on This is a collection of Proverbs that were written and recorded over a span of many years in the life and times of its author. The original intent of theses idioms was for the health, wealth and direction of his children and their future families. Although the author conveys these writings to be original to him in structure, he also concludes that there is absolutely nothing new under the sun. After having recorded over 3,000 truths and faithful sayings, the author decided to publish and share many of them in this topically indexed book.

Introduction

Throughout the pages of this book, you will find answers for many of life's most challenging questions in a short-concise, proverbial form. The author has arranged 31 specific chapters that he believes will cover virtually every topic in question one may have. Each chapter provides a main subject as well as the subject's related antonym, (denoted in parenthesis).

Ecclesiastes 12:9

(9) *And moreover, because the preacher was wise, he still taught the people knowledge; yea, he gave good heed, and sought out, and set in order MANY PROVERBS.*

About the Author

James Warren Bryant (Born October 22nd, 1968) currently serves at the pastorate at Dillon Congregational. James is the son of the church' founders, John L. Bryant Jr. and wife Sarah Ray Bryant and has two siblings, brother, Johnny Ray Bryant and sister, Cynthia Robin Bryant Willoughby. James is also the husband of Marcia (Lynette) Rouse Bryant and father of their three children, Destiny Anne Leggette {Chad Leggette}, Holly Bryant Martin {Josh Martin} and Lily Anna Bryant, and proud Granddaddy of Jack Dawson Leggette.

Some notable aspects of Bryant's ministry while at Dillon Congregational have been the creation of their own unique Logo. It was designed in the early 2000's by Bryant to convey a message of distinction as to their location as well as their main biblical scripture source.

James Bryant was also responsible for the church' Community Charities birth that would benefit organizations such as the American Cancer Society, American

Red Cross and others. Along with friend and former Dillon County Chamber of Commerce President, Robert Earl Johnson, Bryant Co-founded & Co-Chaired the Annual Dillon County Car Show event launched 2005. Through the love of American Muscle Cars (especially Ford Mustangs), Bryant was able to witness Christ Jesus to his friend Robert and win him to the lord. On Monday, March 20th, 2006 @ 1:10pm Robert made a profession of faith. Robert and James friendship grew into a more genuine closeness and love for one another that their entire community noticed and still remembers today.

James became sole Chair of the Annual Dillon County Car Show event in 2015 as Robert battled health related issues that would lead to his death on Sunday, August 30th, 2015. James learned the news of Robert's passing immediately following his evening sermon and would have the pleasure of sharing the eulogy at his friend's funeral.

In 2019, during the 15th Annual Car Show event, the City of Dillon, along with the strong support of Mayor, Todd Davis, paid Tribute to both Bryant and Johnson for their birthing of the annual Dillon County Car Show by placing Pavers on the Street of Main with their names displayed as well as their likeness prominently displayed in a silhouette.

Other annual events launched by Bryant include Summer Festivals, as well as the annual Community Charities Sing-Fling Gospel Concerts event launched in 2005 used to benefit youth related charities of Dillon

County. Bryant is also responsible for the birth of his church' annual Van Driver's Appreciation Day (each October) & Sunday School Teacher's Appreciation Day (each January), and other such events. Bryant launched the beginning of everything Internet for his church and is responsible for virtually everything today Media related and recorded.

His work at Dillon Congregational also allowed for his audio skills creativity in recording, editing and releasing various audio and video projects. Bryant's creativity was also utilized in producing and recording both the audio & video renderings of sermons preached behind the pulpit of Dillon Congregational. His efforts allowed parishioners of the church, and admirers from afar, to relive these messages and in so doing he also made a way for future generations to continue to share with many others yet to come.

Bryant sought to preserve the history of Dillon Congregational and digitized thousands of hard copy photos from as early as 1974 and has currently amassed nearly 20,000 pictures in their historical archives. He converted over 850-analog audio cassette tapes from past classic recordings into WAV and or MP3 formatted digital files. These audio recordings consist of sermons, special songs, Sunday School lessons, special services and one on one interviews from a vast number of contributors. All analog (VHS) videos that were retrieved were converted to digital formatted files as well. Following the renovations of the vestibule in the fall of 2012, the church launched a 24/7 feed of the archival pictorial, audio and video recordings edited and created by Bryant onto a 42-inch LCD screen. Much of this recorded history (Pictures, Sermons, Singing) is available to the public today via Internet as well as hardware devices.

Bryant has served the Congregational Holiness Church Inc.' East Carolina District in many capacities that include Presbytery Member, Secretary, Assistant Secretary, Newsletter Editor, Webmaster and Gospel Messenger Reporter.

In the early 2000's Bryant decided to suspend much of his denominational administrative efforts and placed more of his focus on the maturing of his local church and the giving of himself more within' his community.

Bryant has authored and published three books prior to this his fourth, "Think on This."

Endorsements

Rev. Bryant has formulated an amazing set of truths which will take some time to digest. It has been said that if one reads an article in "the journal of clinical investigation" at greater than 25 words a minute, one will fail to comprehend the composition. I have found that Rev. Bryant's book requires much longer attention to assimilate the full meaning of his statements. His thoughts seem to require a query demanding further research and reflection. In a way it is like gazing in a rainbow and appreciating each offering of color differentiation. In my opinion, not to be Peru's over a weekend, but it is a constant source and guidance for one's life's endeavors.

James Suggs M.D.
MUSC Health – Primary Care, Marion SC, Retired

A proverb is defined as: "sayings that express effectively commonplace truths and useful thoughts." Pastor, James W. Bryant has compiled a book of 3,000 proverbs which are drawn from a life and ministry of experience. These life pictures provoke one to give time to thought, and to find answers too many areas of life. In his collection of useful thoughts, Bro. James provides encouragement, healing, warning and inspiration in thirty-one areas of life. It's a good read, it's a worth-while read.

James S. Smith
East Dillon Baptist Church, Senior Pastor

'Think on This' is a timeless treasure that will comfort and motivate readers to navigate this difficult path called life. James Bryant is a true servant in a family lineage of Christian Leaders that have a heart for leading folks to Christ!

Rodney Berry
City of Marion SC, Mayor

This book is filled with thought provoking and timeless proverbs that I enjoyed reading and contemplating. You could read this over and over and never absorb all its life lessons. These are truths that relate to every issue in life that we must all deal with at one time or another. Also, I like how the proverbs are given from a Christian viewpoint. I highly recommend reading this for enjoyment and enrichment!

Stephanie David
Davids' Accounting & Tax Service, Owner/CPA

Acknowledgement

A special thanks to my parents and siblings
for their support with this effort.

Dedication

These Proverbs comes from a lifetime of observation of people and nature itself and the conclusions that they have conveyed to me in my life. To me, the importance of understanding a truth is only second to knowing him who is truth. It is my hope that all whom may follow behind my work will be able to benefit from it.

This book is dedicated to my grandson, Jack Dawson Leggette.

~James W. Bryant

Table of Contents

#1

Anger (Calm)

Be ye angry, and sin not: let not the sun go down upon your wrath.

Ephesians 4:26 KJV

o When one isn't getting the point you sometimes must speak more sharply.

o It's never okay to lose one's temper; but neither should it not occasionally be found.

o Actions should never control anger, though anger may be used to control actions.

o Everybody has that one button that can be pushed, but no one should display an entire keypad.

o Anger is to be expressed but constrained.

o Where help isn't accepted hurt is returned.

o Don't chase a dog that doesn't desire to be caught, he'll bite you.

o Anger is stirred by a perceived wrong but should be settled by the obvious right.

o Love doesn't anger, long.

o Love doesn't say not to be in anger, but love will not stay in anger.

o Anger shouldn't be kindled against the preacher who preaches with fire but with the one who only uses smoke.

o A fire not fueled will burn out.

o Anger can be used to fuel flames of warmth or flames of fire.

o If you can't get along, get alone.

o Refraining one's words while filled with anger is for him to hold sand within' the palm of the hand without leakage.

o Emotion both fuels and outs fire.

o Trying to rescue an angry man from his battles is like trying to out a forest fire with a water hose.

o When one does wrong he should think twice.

#2

Character (Dishonesty)

A [good] name [is] rather to be chosen than
great riches, [and] loving favour rather than
silver and gold.

Proverbs 22:1 KJV

o One's best may not always be good enough, but he should always give it.

o Doing the right thing when you have absolutely nothing to gain is most rewarding.

o It's impossible for man to remove what has been put within' him, but it's no excuse for what has to come out of him.

o Man can't help but notice the obvious, but he can choose not to see it.

o What's seen on the outside will fade away, but that which is on the inside shines forever.

o Every day of life is a performance, act well.

o True leadership is shown in how one makes an exit, not merely an entrance.

o Man will show you on the way out, who they truly were on the way in.

o If one doesn't behave, he can still be responsible.

o Endorsements and criticisms both reveal values, campaign well.

o The only thing one will take with him will be what he leaves behind.

o You don't send a message to be right, you be right, and the message will be sent.

o Decision should be made before the question.

o Character is not regulated but rather demonstrated.

o Character should dictate man's action, his action should not dictate his character

o Man will be clothed by whatever thoughts he has in his closet.

o Respect the truth and don't resist it, for if you fail to it will prove to have dishonored you.

o When someone wrongly uses a man's moral character against him, he knows that he has done things right.

o The character of a man doesn't change, he just chooses to reveal it or conceal it.

o The front-page news will often be about the last chapter in the book.

o A good name must be worked for, a bad name comes easily.

o You can hide in truth or be found in a lie.

o Where change has been made, evidence will be seen.

o One mistake doesn't make you a failure; neither does adhering to one truth make you a success.

o It's an easy path to gain temporary favor, but a long road to retain lasting respect.

o The effort to do right should be the only thing one efforts to do.

o A true selfless act will be considerate of others and not merely a sacrifice of self.

o Having the respect of one's family is above every criticism of his enemies.

o Pressure reveals character.

o Just because one's hands are in the right place it doesn't mean that his heart is in the right place.

o Doing good shouldn't be contingent upon someone having done us good.

o One shouldn't expect the benefit of the doubt that doesn't steadily exercise in the practice of the truth.

o The chameleon changes his color to adapt to his surroundings; as does the unprincipled man.

o That which is sneaking in is hard to be run out.

o It is not to do because it is good; it is to do good because it is right.

o The liberal position is supported by those who solely seek to lose accountability.

o The man that pursues being liked by all will be respected by few.

o Where the line is blurred much can be seen.

o It's better not to be the person that you were only if you're the person that you should have been.

o The man of character doesn't always say what's right, but if that man says it, he believes it.

o Although what you do doesn't determine who you are, who you are will determine what you do.

o Composure is challenged by difficulty and achieved by determination.

o Where the proper action has been settled the appropriate reaction can only be stirred.

o Popularity passes, but principles endure.

o Retention is most often held not by what is being said, nor the way one may be saying it, but rather by the man that is saying it.

o Life is to be lived as if under the recording in which we are.

o Man's biography is being written while he lives.

o Poise in adversity reveals much.

o Principal should always come before interest.

o The man that truly loves God, family and Country will serve, provide and defend them.

o The man who has nothing to hide will fear no detection.

o A man's personality doesn't determine his heart.

o Doing right may place you at a disadvantage, but it will lead you to many more advantages.

o Embarrassment reveals the heart.

o Height should be measured from one's depth not their peak.

o One cannot greatly influence another unless he is found to be somewhat different.

o Influence is certain, its effect is questionable.

o Flash without splash is of no effect.

o Charisma without character is worthless.

o Influence is mightier than suggestion.

o Style will change, character will not.

o Composure is the column that holds up Principal.

o It is better to be ate up by the lion than spit out by the den.

o Encroachment is responsible for more loss than can be seen.

o Whatever one lines himself up with that shall he lean.

o As the end comes near, good men become better and bad men become worse.

o In order to go through the door, one must first enter it.

o One cannot be threatened of an exit when he is already on the way out.

o The character of a man can most often be determined by who his heroes are.

o What we do will speak louder than what we say.

o To tolerate is to encourage.

o The greatest treasure that one can leave behind is not his signature, but rather his name.

o A volunteer's service cannot be bought.

o It is better to be criticized for right than to be praised for wrong.

o Good folks make mistakes, better folks make them right.

o It's good to have everything you want, it's better to own everything that you have.

o Conscious efforts to do good will reduce a subconscious response from doing bad.

o The greatest feat of one's strength is its restraint.

o A lifetime of achievements is birthed in a moment of decision.

o The man who never falls is the man that never stands.

o The true values of a man can most often be determined by what he condemns or commends the most.

o A good name is developed not anointed.

o Character is doing right subconsciously.

o Integrity is gained through the loss of foolishness.

o The man that doesn't keep his word will lose his voice.

o One cannot develop character before acquiring problems.

o Character does what bravery cannot.

o Man's character is more often killed by suicide than homicide.

o When one notices an improvement, many have seen the need.

o If you want to change the way you act, change the way you feel. If you want to change the way you feel, change the way you think.

o It is the wise that will do all he can to get along, and the fool that will always go along.

o The hardest person one will ever seek to control is also the only one that he can control.

o The man that cannot be rescued by his efforts can be condemned by his actions.

o Those who are a seen as a fake cannot be heard as real.

o The man that is missed is more visible than the man that is present.

o Doing right is to be fueled by duty not emotion.

o The person that doesn't hold themselves up, let others down.

o Character is a possession desired by all, pursued by many, and paid for by few.

o A loss with integrity is better than a win with corruption.

o Corruption lies down at night and cannot sleep, while integrity has no struggles.

o It is better to leave a good name than to leave a good score.

o Integrity is often condemned but debauchery is always damned.

o A label suggests the contents. So does the man's trademark identify his business.

o The testimony that is being heard is the one that is being shown.

o The man that carries himself well will by others be lifted greatly.

o The loudest noise is preceded first by the biggest bang.

o The biggest building is no greater than its foundation.

o Outcome can only follow income.

o It is more to live what we say, than to merely say how we live.

o The good pastor may be deceived but the better pastor will repent from his error.

o Being polished doesn't change one's self, just others view of them.

o A good perception is often achieved by displaying an image that is always desired.

o When inspiration has been replaced by obligation it will often reveal if it was imitation.

o What we do declares who we are.

o Character is greater revealed in not in how you act, but rather in how you react.

o One is labeled according to the ingredients found within' him.

o If you want to see what something is made out of, just squeeze it.

#3

Courage (Fear)

For God hath not given us the spirit of fear; but of power, and of love, and of a sound mind.

2nd Timothy 1:7 KJV

o Critics criticize because that is what they are supposed to do; do what you are supposed to do.

o If you are not enjoying the conversation, simply hang up the phone.

o Man is not to sling the dirt on anyone; but if he is continually being dumped on himself, he will either respond, or else by it be buried.

o If you don't stand up you won't have to worry about getting knocked down; however, you will likely get stepped on.

o Lessons are not to be merely taught but are also to be reinforced.

o Don't let your fault deny your effort.

o When you don't have a 100% to give, give a 100% of what you got.

o Man can never be good, but he can always do good.

o The compromises in life that we should strive for is not that which is politically correct, but rather that which is right.

o Courage isn't pretending to be something that God didn't make; courage is accepting what God has made you for.

o One is stepped on simply because he doesn't get up.

o People will out your fire or either fuel it, its outcome is all up to you.

o Don't just play a role, commit to a part.

o Be driven not pulled.

o Being of a valiant personality is the best thing since sliced bread to others when they are hungry; but when they are full audaciousness is impossible to be swallowed.

o Scared is faster than courage.

o An axe will indeed take a tree down, but a chainsaw just feels better doing it.

o Courage isn't being strong; it's not letting weakness stop you.

o Personality can be deceiving but the man of principle will not hide.

o A will is greater than a way.

o While remaining in neutral may not get you in to any-thing, neither will it get you out.

o Where choice isn't available, preferred should be demanded.

o It's easier to side with wrong than to stand for right.

o The man that never falls has never stood.

o Uncertainty causes one not to show his position, but the bold will write it down.

o Life isn't necessarily easy, but the answers are basi-cally simple.

o Life is full of simple answers; don't be complicated by the questions.

o The truth seasoned is often swallowed more easily, but the nose is to be held where its serving is needed and being avoided.

o The best response to chaos is calmness.

o Man's environment shouldn't change him, he should change his environment.

o The lack of restraint separates.

o Reason if you can, suggest if you cannot; demand if you must, apply if you continue.

o Politicians reflect the voice of the people; leaders express the words of God.

o The quickest way around trouble is right through the middle.

o It's better to get knocked down than to have never been known to stand up.

o Terrorism is foiled by heroism.

o If one doesn't stop that which is creeping up, it will soon be sneaking in.

o Two things that hinder the preacher from preaching. Sin in his life and or sin in his members.

o Hunger feeds courage.

o The greatest measure of toughness is to be determined by what one can take.

o Pressure is birthed from the fear of failure.

o Moses would have never crossed the red sea if he hadn't first seen a need to move towards it.

o In order to get to the other side, one must first wade out into the middle.

o The only people that can be moved by being pushed are the ones who are moveable.

o You can't stop a storm, but you can prepare for it.

o The only thing you can lose by doing nothing is everything.

o When most become outnumbered they generally either change position or change addresses.

o The act of change is one's greatest accomplishment or his worse demise.

o The greatest travesty in life is to know that the end is coming, and not be prepared for it.

o The man who has nothing to lose also has everything to gain.

o What can't be stopped can be refused.

o Where no line is drawn there can be no separation. Neither can there be any distinction in right from wrong without a stance.

o Seeing an exit always eases one's entrance.

o Will is stronger than might.

o What fear suggests courage will deny.

o Decisions made today will affect the outcome of tomorrow.

o Restraint takes more strength than excursion.

o The only man that cannot change is the man who will not change.

o Where no side is given, neither is any taken.

o The troublemaker is branded as the man that disturbs the system, but it is the fool that always goes along with it.

o Failure will motivate the good man to succeed.

o The good man experiences lapse not collapse.

o With the right to make a mistake comes the duty to make those mistakes right.

o Men are made or broken by challenge.

o When one's values are being tested they will not be weakened, but strengthened.

o The good man will be willing to stand up for his political party, as well as stand up to his political party.

o God has called man to be the salt of the earth, not the sweetener.

o Fear is a tactic, not a determiner.

o If you give it your best, you will better be able to take the worst.

#4

Family (Ancestry)

(For if a man know not how to rule his own house, how shall he take care of the church of God?)

1st Timothy 3:5 KJV

17

o God has ordered the family to carry out his agenda. The objective of Satan is to destroy what God has set in order.

o More consideration should be given to babies in the womb than terrorist on the battlefield.

o Don't send your kids to Jesus, take them.

o Evil pushes man to do the grave sins that he does, but faith in Christ and commitment to the family pulls him from it and will prevent much.

o Making fond memories can be just as rewarding as reliving them.

o The best investment that a parent can make to their society is in the lives of his or her children.

o No government can hold up where its values on family have been let down.

o Kids can be challenging; parents can be impossible.

o The single biggest cause for the leap of children being born out of wedlock is the safety-net of welfare.

o Where there's a steady presence of a father there will be a greater absence of hunger.

o A home united can conquer a world divided.

o A parent is not to be valued most by the good that he tries to give to his children, but rather by the bad that he attempts to keep from them.

o The greatest blessing a parent can give to his children is a disciplined life walked in integrity.

o Those who do well when they are grown must be taught well while they are small.

o Everything that is found wrong in a society can be fixed by what is made right in the family.

- A parent's wisdom is not merely to be read but should be subscribed to.

- A child should never mature beyond his parent's council.

- The young man is to be broken by restraints, managed by rules or else loosed to fail.

- The most important institution that a man will ever be a part of is his home.

- It is the abusive parent who refuses to discipline their child.

- It is an abuse not to discipline children.

- Only the parent can understand love as it relates to a child.

- The father that does not rule his own house well will be well taken by his own home.

- The amount of discipline should be measured only by the amount of disobedience.

- Perfect children are seen by flawed parents.

- The good father will not praise his child unworthily, for the parent who does will only prepare the child for failure.

- Little will hurt you more than that which you love the most.

- What good is a man that will do his job on Monday but lay out of work the rest of the week? So is the man that is not faithful to his home.

- The one that will not mind his parents does not regard his children.

o Silliness and perverseness is a sickness of every child; but the way of the switch is often the means to a cure.

5

Forgiveness (Blame)

And when ye stand praying, forgive, if ye have ought against any: that your Father also which is in heaven may forgive you your trespasses.

Mark 11:25 KJV

o Everybody will get into it; nobody should stay into it.

o Failing to admit failure falters finding forgiveness.

o There are more hangings that take place from the pulpit than has there ever any Government gallows.

o Why should one be surprised with what comes up if by his own hand the seed was planted?

o Being right doesn't give permission to do wrong.

o Bitterness sours.

o Whatever man misplaces is generally right where he left it.

o Where excuses go long answers will come short.

o It's not so much the ignorance of a people that is responsible, but more so those that know better that allow their ignorance.

o An apology not given with the same vigor to restore all restitution is hardly an apology.

o Crying foul smells.

o Forgiveness can begin the healing, but blame will prolong any injury.

o A chip on the shoulder comes from a splinter of the head.

o You cannot be close to anyone without getting bumped once and a while.

o Forgiveness should be sought and expressed with the same vigor as the sin that prompted it.

o When complaining becomes comfortable, content-ment then becomes inconceivable.

o Those who are offended by others whom they say are judging, are they not then themselves judging and causing offense?

o Being bitter prevents one from becoming better.

o Forgiveness is a release from capture.

o Dispensation doesn't demand association but merely an end of blame.

o The only sinner not guilty is the pardoned.

o The measure of mercy that man extends often determines the measure of mercy that he receives.

o The greatest wounds are self-inflicted.

o It is impossible to defend self without offending others.

o Forgiveness is only a request away.

o Equality is to be defined by every man having a voice, not by the outcome coming out equal.

o One's confession needs only be towards those to whom it is due.

o Grace makes worthy the unworthy and unworthy the worthy.

o The surest cure for a bad memory is amnesia.

o You fight fire with fire. You out fire with water.

o Being guilty doesn't condemn, not being pardoned does.

o The one thing in the next life that you cannot escape is judgment.

o There is nothing wrong that cannot be made right.

o Wrong can be forgiven, but evil will not seek it.

o When enthusiasm has been taken it is impossible to give it back.

#6

Freedom (Bondage)

But whoso looketh into the perfect law of liberty, and continueth [therein], he being not a forgetful hearer, but a doer of the work, this man shall be blessed in his deed.

James 1:25 KJV

o Without safety and security there can be no pursuit of happiness.

o A crutch feels good to lean on, but you will never run with it.

o You don't escape from whom you were, you force him along with you.

o Where the ability to bully one is given, the ability to bully many will be taken.

o The heart of a society is not its current administration, but the pulse of its people.

o Where integrity is lost tyranny is found.

o Nothing but the word of God opens the blinded eye, causes the lame to walk, and the dumb to talk. But a Smith & Wesson comes close.

o Democracy doesn't assure accuracy but does define ultimate blame.

o The man who fights to take away the freedoms of others only enslaves himself.

o There's no way to keep from getting mixed up in a thing that is steadily stirring. The only way to come clean is to be removed from that environment.

o God allows man to choose his own desires but prohibits him from selecting the consequences. He lives however with them both.

o Ability cannot disable what authority has enabled.

o The free man chooses well his own captivity.

o It takes an education to end a war, but merely an idiot to launch one.

o Employment is not rescued by the imprisonment of the Employer.

o Where there's an absence of family values there will be a presence of national turmoil.

o Where there is no restraint there can be no freedom.

o The soul that is grieving with guilt will be absent of fellowship.

o The man that is freed from slavery isn't long enslaved by his freedom.

o Freedom is given by permission.

o To escape jail doesn't merit one's own lack of guilt.

o The heart can be changed but the mind cannot be escaped.

o While water does cleanse the soil, it also muddies the water.

o There is no speech to be considered where the voice is not heard.

o One can only govern what the government allows to be governed.

o When the floor is given up, the walls are taken down.

o One should always seek for peace but prepare for war.

o The right to life, liberty and the pursuit of happiness ends where Pro-abortion begins.

o Societies can be policed only as much as they allow themselves to be governed.

o A bad habit is as strong as a new prison to be broken.

#7

Friendship (Enemies)

Faithful [are] the wounds of a friend; but the kisses of an enemy [are] deceitful.

Proverbs 27:6 KJV

o Ugliness ceases when it's no longer in your view.

o Opposition isn't concerned that you're going to fail, it is scared that you're going to succeed.

o A broken trust is hard to be fixed, but a proven loyalty should be impossible to break.

o Sometimes it's better to simply bury the living and keep alive the dead.

o Don't forsake your longtime proven friends so quickly; and don't be too quick to give all your heart to those you've only known briefly.

o Pray for your friends, and for your enemies.

o To the faithful, loyalty matters; to matters, few are faithful.

o A friend will first get in your ear; an enemy will first get in the ear of others.

o A liquid of any color is still a liquid.

o A friend will prefer to talk to you in private, not desire to blow you up in public.

o An acquaintance will want to see you do well; a friend will want to see you do better.

o The measure of friendships shouldn't be restricted by the amount of another's income but should be more so defined by your input's outcome.

o If one has your best interest at heart, they will endeavor to place only God's truth into your ear.

o All of man falls short but it is the evil man who seeks to pull others down with them.

o A friend will be in your ear, an enemy will be in the ear of someone else.

o Three kinds of people that will be in one's life; those who lean towards you, with you, or against you.

o Preservatives lengthen the life of any food, so does good deeds the life of every relationship.

o A faultless friend cannot be found, nor will one ever be found searching.

o Be slow to add and slower to subtract.

o Friendships can change, but those who endure all will remain.

o Crisis reveals friends from masqueraders.

o A friend will rebuke your wrong, but it is the deceiver who always goes along.

o Wish well towards others so that others may wish well towards you.

o Anyone that you must constantly chase, you don't need to continue to catch.

o Conflicts are certain, outcomes are questionable.

o You can't lose one whom never was a friend.

o The one that pins you out on a clothesline will live you there to dry.

o Not every friend is going to meet your every need but value the need that is being met by your every friend!

o Forsaking a friendship is purchasing a mistake that you can't easily afford.

o Those who are a cited as target are also considered as a threat.

o A truthful friend is a priceless treasure, but the deceptive enemy will cost you much.

o Its difficult outing fires when you don't know who is striking the matches.

o Political affiliation should align with one's values, not one with theirs.

o When you can no longer feed the lion, you become the food.

o You can tell who one is truly following by watching the steps that they are continually walking.

o A man's life is shaped by the hands of those who surround him.

o Do not run after what God removes from you.

o Before each split there must first come a wedge.

o An acquaintance will desire for his friend to do well, but a friend will desire for his acquaintance to do better.

o God is all that is needed, but a friend fulfills a lot of want.

o Loyalty is easily seen but rarely shown.

o The one that has to say that they have your back is often the one that is after your throat.

o The friend that hurts you can help you, the friend that helps you can hurt you.

o A proven friend is to be appreciated, while they last.

o A friend loves at all time, but not necessarily always will one be a friend.

o The Lord often supplies our strength through the efforts of our friends.

o Individual strength grouped together greatly lessens weakness.

o The preacher is to be a friend of the sinner but an enemy to his enemy's sin.

o Happiness is returned from where it is given.

o Regularity dulls what's wrong and or strengthens what is right.

o The advances of a friend should often be to retreat.

o Strong suspicions are motivated by slight reactions.

o Small gestures make giant influences.

o A real friend may not be around you the most, but a real friend will be there when you need them the most.

o Friendship forgives foolishness.

o Friendship forgives fault.

o The same one that stands with you today will likely side against you tomorrow.

o You will get along with only as many as you're willing to put up with.

o A bullet is of no use without a weapon, and the weapon is of no harm without a host.

o More friends produce fewer enemies.

o Life's greatest favors are often given by their friend, Judas.

o When one feels that they can no longer talk to you, they will then begin to talk about you.

o A man who hasn't any enemies is a man who has many victims.

o The best way to keep a close friend is to keep them at a good distance.

o The ones walking away from you often want to be caught but the ones running from you don't.

o The man without legs cannot run one down.

o The problem with buying friends is that you will have to pay for it.

o An enemy will quickly remind you as to why they're not your friend.

o It's not that friends won't hurt you, but when they realize they make it right.

o A step backwards is sometimes made to merely camouflage a step forward.

o A man's actions can be misleading, but his reactions are more often revealing.

o True friends can often be counted on one finger, if you're lucky.

o Jealousy often hides behind friendships but is exposed through hardships.

o Wealth reveals many friends while poverty hides man from them.

o Having a bad neighbor is like having a good enemy; neither is of worth nor want.

o A true friend will enlighten you to try and be of a help; while a deceitful enemy will inform you to try and be of a help to his self.

o What doesn't come naturally must be taught.

o A good neighbor is hard to find, and a bad neighbor is hard to lose.

o Beware of the man who will tell you only what you want to hear; for that man only seeks to profit from your losses.

o Nothing brings opposing men together tighter than the fear from them both of being torn apart.

o The path of the least resistance leads to the road of the most acceptances.

o The deceiver often wears a smile to mask his intentions.

o Miles can separate friends, but no distance can divide friendship.

o The ones finding fault of others not visiting enough, would find fault in their length of stay if they had.

o Chasing and individual who does not want to be caught only tires you from being able to catch those that do.

o Having a bad neighbor is like having a good sickness.

o To confront the scornful of his ways is to step on the tail of the dog.

o When the one that you trusted has hurt you, God will provide another to heal you.

o Every close friend will have their faults, but they're worth it.

o An acquaintance will be glad to see you doing good for you. A friend will be happy even when you're doing better than them.

o It is better to have a genuine enemy than a fake friend.

o It's hard to know a real friend while times are easy, but easy to know a real friend when times are hard.

o Jealousy reveals resentment in those who see you as a rival.

o A loving neighbor is more to be desired than a disdainful relative.

o   If the only time you hear from a friend is when they use that opportunity to elevate themselves and or discredit you, they just might not be a friend.

o   Even light, cast among obstacles, will cast shadows: Consider greatly your surroundings.

#8

Generosity (Stinginess)

There is that scattereth, and yet increaseth; and [there is] that withholdeth more than is meet, but [it tendeth] to poverty.

The liberal soul shall be made fat: and he that watereth shall be watered also himself.

Proverbs 11:24-25

o There can be no investment without a contribution; Give to that you might receive from.

o The Christian won't want for need, but his need may want from won't.

o You never see the measure of real value being made on your investments in another, but it is satisfying when and if you can only get a peek.

o What good is the boat that can go to the deepest part of the ocean that never leaves the dock? For it is greater to be small and eagerly move about in the shallows, than to be huge and never wet a hook.

o No sight is more pleasurable than the view of happiness in the eye of whom you've pleasured.

o Man shouldn't do to get, but rather get to do.

o Every man should be expected to give, but no man should be governed to do so.

o Those with a heart of gold are too often excavated of it by others.

o The line of those in need will always exceed the line of those willing to help.

o One shouldn't expect to draw more from the pitcher than they have poured into it.

o Man has the right to pursue happiness in his own labor not the entitlement to find it at his neighbor's expense.

o A right is wrong when it's claimed on another man's wallet.

o Supporting others strengthens self.

o If you want to receive help, be a help.

o Man's value should be calculated by what he gives not what he has received.

o Success should be measured by what you give, not by what you get.

o Entitlement promotes unemployment.

o No one should be given the right of choice to take from another who has no choice.

o Liberal values should reflect conservative principals.

o To please everyone is to deceive self.

o The second greatest gift one can give or receive is time.

o It is easier on the giver to give when the getter that receives appreciates that which is got.

o Man's greatest weaknesses come from the toils of labor that are spent while serving him.

o Pleasing favors preference.

o One sure way to receive a blessing is to first be a blessing.

o The man that complains about having to do for others should first consider that others could be having to do for him.

o By continuing to do the unexpected it will become expected.

#9

Hope (Despair)

For we are saved by hope: but hope that is seen is not hope: for what a man seeth, why doth he yet hope for?

Romans 8:24 KJV

o Hatred indeed stirs up great evil, but faith in God (with works), restores order and calming peace.

o Getting a little excited doesn't make one holy; holiness is only found in Christ.

o If anytime would not be a good time for you for the Lord to return, you are probably right.

o Hope doesn't quit; don't quit on hope.

o A lot of songs that suggest holding on should be cut loose.

o There are many gods but only one God.

o The pulpit should do less trying to get the saved lost and more trying to get the lost saved.

o The only line the saved man cannot cross is grace.

o God doesn't forsake his people; those who forsake God never were his people.

o One's daddy may forsake him, but not his Father.

o The only one you can trust with your salvation is Christ Jesus.

o One that can see can be blind, but the one that is blind cannot see.

o Those who are saved will endure to the end.

o If you don't have a desire in your life to serve the lord, you probably don't have the lord in your life to serve.

o The heart that will not change cannot be changed.

o Anything short of grace is a disgrace.

o The branch may droop, it may even be cut back; but wherever there's a root there will surely come a shoot.

o It's not that the boogieman is going to get you if you've been bad but rather, if you've not been saved.

o "If ye continue," is not a benchmark that man is to work to achieve, it is the reality of if he was ever there.

o One should not be ashamed of holiness but should be ashamed of what some make it out to be.

o When it's out of our control it's still under God's control.

o Works cannot get you into heaven; neither can the lack thereof keep you from it.

o Having a different view out of the window doesn't change your destination, so long as you have the same driver.

o Evil is at work, but God owns the business.

o No matter what position some may put you in; God can send another and deliver you.

o If your hope is hopeless, remain hopeful and get another hope.

o Hope isn't an absence of trouble; it is the presence of overcoming.

o Faith will keep one on point even when it hurts.

o Andrew didn't lead three thousand to Christ, he led one.

o In this life, there cannot be any good without the bad. In the next life, there can't be any bad with the good.

o Ensure your assurance.

o When we're at our lowest sometimes God sends an angel to remind us of him who is highest.

o Assurance is better than insurance, for it doesn't promise hope it is hope.

o You can't always be where God is, but he will always be where you are.

o You can't fight everybody and win, let God help you.

o To wait upon his return is to continue in the journey.

o The one who is not always right need only trust in the one who is never wrong.

o Man is a spirit that is born before birth, a voice without words while he is alive, and a life without body after he is dead.

o You may not be able to go back to where you were, but you can always go forward from where you are.

o Find enjoyment in today and look for it in tomorrow.

o Gravity centers all that is around a man; it is from his core, not covering, that he finds balance.

o True life is more of a philosophy than it is a science. For science must be proven, but belief only hoped.

o Godly faith isn't something that you merely willing to live for but more so that in which you're willing to die for.

o Having faith in God doesn't guarantee deliverance in this life but looking unto Jesus assures one of salvation in the next one.

o Where faith has been established works will be erected.

o Faith is not void of doubt but is full of hope.

o If in this life this was all that there was, then in all would be nothing in this life that is.

o Hope is pavement for the road that leads to and intended destination.

o Everyone has problems, few accept the answer.

o Those that endure spiritual storms shall reign in celestial heavens.

o Prayer may not change God to whom man speaks, but prayer is certain to change the man who speaks to God.

o Worrying won't rob tomorrow's problems but it will steal today's answers.

o With each new day comes the potentiality to begin a new life.

o The good preacher is willing to chance our better despite the possibility of our worse.

o The future can be re-written, but history cannot be erased.

o The man, who has nothing but salvation, has everything.

o At its worse it can only get better for the child of God.

o The man that can't go back doesn't have to stay where he is, he can always go forward.

o The man that can take the bad news is the man who has already been given the good news.

o It isn't over when it's over; it's merely a time to resurrect.

o Being at peace or at war with God will determine man's comfort or lack thereof.

o The most miserable person in the room is the one cornered of self.

o The best way to feel better about self is to consider others.

o Exercising faith strengthens hope.

o Dominos successes are found in their failure, so is man's hope found in his own hopelessness.

o Where there is no hope there is no help.

- o Patience plus faith produces hope.
- o False hope is better than true despair.
- o The one with nothing to lose has a lot to gain.
- o The difference in failing and a failure is one keeps on trying and the other one quits.
- o More is to be profited at arguing with God than with the devil.
- o A Dream is a vehicle that takes us to our past, present and or our future.
- o Dreams bring sight while asleep, but clarity varies by the dreamer.
- o The clearest vision often comes through closed eyes.
- o Where's there's breath, there's hope.
- o A seed is only as good as the ground that it falls upon.
- o Though one may not be able to change his past, he can alter his future.
- o Immortal Life is found in the surrender to escape Mortal Death.
- o The one thing of this world that you can count on is that there's nothing of this world that you can count on.
- o What can't be chosen can be rejected.
- o Darkness provides a greater opportunity to shine.
- o While man's nature seeks to destroy him, his spirit seeks for a savior.
- o Achieved expectations yield relief, while hope unveils joy.
- o When the perfect person has been found all hope has then been lost.

o If you miss it on everything but Jesus you've made it. If you make it on everything but Jesus, you will miss it.

o The only thing more important than one's physical health is his spiritual condition.

o When we remove and disregard biblical teachings from our society their can and will be no restraint of true morality within' our communities.

o Christian values are not defined by color but rather by the plain words of God.

o One must position himself close to the book so that he can remove himself far from the sins.

o Where one's thoughts dwell, his actions follow.

o To properly prepare for doomsday is not to store up everything but to prepare to leave everything.

o Christ may come to some at different levels, but he is ultimately the only elevator ride to the top.

o Works will not get a man saved, but the saved man is to maintain good works.

o The man who makes God's glory his end will not lose his way.

o Faith demands action.

o Seizing the moment requires faith for the future.

o Sin is to break the law; evil is to have no sorrow in it.

o Not one thing of this world can save man, but everything in it can damn him.

o It's not the man doing the preaching, but rather the preaching being done by the man.

o If Christ had not went through what he had, we couldn't go through what we could.

o When all fails you, the word will lift you.

o If we are being held up by Jesus, we cannot be let down by others.

o Man doesn't live right to get right; he gets right to live right.

o Man's outcome is not determined by the weight in which he is under but rather by his ability or inability to handle it.

o To believe in a thing is to have faith in it.

o Faith is revealed best by through works accomplished.

o If a man is going to walk right, he will need his head on straight.

o Devotion delivers distinctive direction.

o We need only confess our sins regularly to wash our souls constantly.

o Revival services shouldn't make you spiritual but rather scheduled. For if a man will schedule it, he can remain spiritual.

o Spiritual notifications which cannot be seen or heard can be interpreted.

o The lack of faith produces the fear of failure while a bounty of faith results in an assurance of success.

o Christ is captured where Faith is loosed.

o If we've taken care of our history, we will not need to be as concerned about our future.

o For every Stephen stoned there will be another Paul constructed.

o Times of difficulty are made more comfortable to those who please God.

o Man's ultimate success doesn't come by his own hand but rather through God's touch.

o Acceptance isn't always according to our merits but according to God's favor.

o Heavenly sent revival falls from hell shaking prayer.

o When we lose self, we find God.

o Fun without Christ will always end in sadness.

o Collective salvation is damned.

o Those that pray in faith will rejoice in hope.

o One is ill-equipped to live until he has prepared to die.

o Adversity strains faith to reveal its truth.

o If man's certainty isn't much worth dying for it isn't much worth living for.

o Nothing of this world can fill the space for that which is designed for what is not of this world.

o The Spirit of God will move when he is stirred.

o When you come as you are you will leave who you were.

o Death is either a confinement or an escape but not an ending.

o Sanctification prevents perversion not salvation.

o Salvation removes the guilt of man's sins but not the sins from man's nature.

o Salvation doesn't remove man from sin but rather sin from man.

o The grace of Christ' blood is only found where it has been applied.

o Sin does not keep you out of heaven, not being saved from those sins will.

o The means of worship from all may vary, but the one being worshiped by all should not.

o The worst place to put God in one's life is second.

o Life is short. Don't wait too long.

o The most important thing in life is to be prepared for death.

o There are many helpers but only one Savior.

o True worship is not limited to being emotional but is the inspiration of the displaying of that affection.

o There is no weight too heavy for man to carry where God is found as his strength.

o The sinner is waiting to die, while the saint is preparing to live.

o Faith is more important than knowledge.

o A state of negative circumstances is an opportunity for positive outcome.

o Our strength is not found in our might, but rather in our measure of belief in Almighty God.

o Faith is belief being exercised.

o A new suit on an old man doesn't ensure change, but a new man in an old suit assures it.

o You can't jump a ditch without taking a leap.

o Though hope can be changed by fact, fact can be changed by faith.

o There's a vast difference in believing in a thing and following a thing.

o When you know who God is, it no longer matters who you are.

o If the rapture is the question, the days that will follow will be the exclamation point.

o If the rapture is the hidden question of the moment, then the days that will follow will unveil the exclamation point.

o Being saved should lead others to Jesus, not point them there.

o If you don't live right, you will die wrong.

o When man has a big vision of God, he will have a small vision of self.

o The most important thing that you can do in this life is to prepare for the next one. The second most important thing is to help prepare someone else.

o One must do right in order not to get left.

o Faithful people are not looking for excuses but are revealing the answers.

o The mind is a filter to the heart and the heart is the reservoir of our flow.

o The believer without fruits is like an angel without wings.

o Eternal hope beyond amazing grace is forever hopeless.

o Physical blood causes man to die while spiritual blood causes man to live.

o Christ in your heart is seen brighter than a pendant around your neck.

o The repentance of God is a change of divine purpose, while the repentance of man is a change of eternal direction.

- o God cannot lie though his direction can change, while man can change though his nature can still lie.
- o When all you have is the Word, it will do.
- o True revival doesn't begin by marking a calendar, but rather by selecting today's date.
- o Belief has no need in being displayed as its proclamation will be reflected and that without effort.
- o Outward worship merely demonstrates inner affection.
- o You can't lose if you've already won.

#10

Jealousy (Admiration)

Thou shalt not covet thy neighbour's house, thou shalt not covet thy neighbour's wife, nor his manservant, nor his maidservant, nor his ox, nor his ass, nor any thing that [is] thy neighbour's.

Exodus 20:17 KJV

o Where bitterness has been tasted sourness will be found.

o Jealousy is often camouflaged but rarely hidden.

o The man who is down to his soles and sandals that is being critical of another with much, is just as guilty of profiting; the only difference is measure.

o To enjoy the failures of others should reveal the failures of self.

o A slight leverage is more powerful than the greatest strength.

o Vengeance often follows jealousies.

o Praising completes that in which one truly delights.

o Conceived blessings have birthed a many of curse.

o Jealousy robs joy.

o Jealousy wears many masks but hides only one face.

o A dirty mind is jealous of a clean conscious.

o Jealousy is often found behind every front.

o When fault can't be found a trap then is likely to be set.

o The one who is doing a little better shouldn't be treated a little worse.

o Influence weakens and or strengthens.

o The man that cannot enjoy his neighbor's blessings only burdens himself with a curse.

o Love envies not the honors received by others, but ill-will is grieved at their every advance.

o What a man doesn't have doesn't entitle him to take from someone who does.

o Those that pour out lies are merely filled with jealousies.

o Respect always follows truth, while admiration is often lead by deceit.

o Opposition proceeds advancement.

o Those who succeed in the building of character are hated by those who choose not.

o Jealousy prompts contempt.

o The man that is master over much will be assuredly condemned by many.

o Every second generation is desired by the first.

o Those that excel in gain will be hated by those who exceed in loss.

#11

Joy (Depression)

A merry heart doeth good [like] a medicine:
but a broken spirit drieth the bones.

Proverbs 17:22 KJV

o Joy can be found where gladness has been stolen.

o Nothing replaces the word of God as the Spiritual nutritional source, but songs of praise provide good seasoning.

o If we suffer for Christ' sake in this life, we will glory with Christ in the next life.

o Living in the enjoyment is not the same as enjoying that in which you're living.

o More emphasis is to be placed on the promoting of the good than the exposing of the bad.

o The Christian's news headline shouldn't contain the hell that he is going through but rather the heaven that he is going to.

o Where delight depends on happiness disenchantment is sure to follow.

o The greatest gift that can be given is to leave an anonymous one

o The dissatisfied seek after either pleasure and or security, the satisfied has it.

o Fun must be fed, but joy feeds on itself.

o When you take all the play out of it, then there's no fun left in it.

o One can never be truly happy until he is truly content.

o The sounds of music often silence the noises of complaint.

o The cause of backsliding begins when the enjoyment of ministry ends.

o You cannot enjoy doing right until you have done right.

o If you only serve God out of joy you will soon sorrow and quit.

o The only satisfaction found is in being satisfied.

o The key to happiness is found at the door of contentment.

o The saint that returns to folly returns to misery.

o The one that keeps things interesting does not get bored.

#12

Justice (Corruption)

[It is] joy to the just to do judgment: but destruction [shall be] to the workers of iniquity.

Proverbs 21:15 KJV

- To love your neighbor as yourself is not to give him everything you've worked for, but rather to have enabled him those same opportunities.
- Being sneaky may get one by longer, but it won't get one by.
- It's not what is being shown that should alarm you the most, but what isn't.
- Incidents should be investigated, not exploited.
- Where there is no resistance there should be no persistence.
- Bad makes good difficult, not impossible.
- All challenges of life should begin with a turning to God and a seeking for his will. Aside from his help, ultimately there can be none.
- One bad person can ruin a lot of good, and one good person can stop a lot of bad.
- Some are selling, some are buying, and some are inventorying.
- With radicals, it only matters when it furthers the cause.
- Murdering is not in the hand, it's in the heart. Defense is not in the heart, it's in the hand.
- Neither man's rights nor his last rites can save him from his wrongs.
- Rebellion is often credited where response has been given.
- The only way to convict the righteous is to outlaw their faith.

o A Government that doesn't want to see their citizens succeed is simply due to the fact they want to keep those citizens dependent, period.

o Only a corrupt government would seek to condemn a political leader for investigating possible corruption.

o A government that is dealing with one that always operates outside the rules cannot be expected to always operate inside the rules.

o Often where no wrong of truth can be found, the truth is then merely wronged.

o Swift justice would slow evil.

o Justice isn't always swift, but it's always certain; God issues it.

o A criminal that believes a crime is worth the risks has too many rights.

o Motive may be hidden from man, but the heart is exposed before the Lord.

o False accusers get away with what they do only because they are allowed.

o A rapid response is not to stop and wait for the police, a rapid response is to be able to go and defend you.

o Don't believe every accusation hear, and don't deny any truth that you see.

o False claims produce unjust harm, but every deceiver will be judged.

o Law don't make right, but every wrong will be judged.

o Men need not fear what he can see but should rather be casting light on those projecting illusions.

o Everybody deserves a chance; nobody should be entitled to assurance.

o Shoot the killer; that always ends alleged gun violence.

o No law that punishes the law-abiding people is a good law.

o Policies preponderate personality, or should.

o Evil will get away with it only if evil can get away with it.

o Discrimination is not an ugly word, using it unjustly is: Just is what God says it is, not how man chooses to discriminate it.

o The greatest fear of the liberal agenda is that its dependents will become independent.

o Political violence removes national doubt.

o When having a preference becomes a crime the law makers will have broken it.

o One can't predict the evil of a man's way, but the 2nd Amendment allows us to be able to stop him.

o Front line combat should not be assigned by political correctness but rather by military readiness.

o Adding weakness to strength subtracts success.

o Man doesn't need more control laws; he needs stronger abuse penalties.

o An umpire's job is to call balls and strikes not pitch them. So are a nation's judges to affirm the law, not re-write it.

o A government's authority should be to merely stress what God's law has already expressed, nothing more.

o Diplomacy more often comes in small steps, not giant leaps.

o Unjust offense is to be avoided, but compromising truth is not to be tolerated.

o Fairness is motivated by truth, but every injustice will be stirred with hypocrisy.

o Lawlessness can tempt divisiveness, but special treatment will assure it.

o A stolen kiss can be forgiven, but ravaged rape should never again be made possible.

o Advancing a false narrative reveals true intent.

o Lawlessness can tempt divisiveness, but special treatment will assure it.

o Equal rights shouldn't include special privileges.

o One should be penalized for his choice not his condition.

o Where penalty is great crime will be small.

o Getting on board late may keep one's feet from getting wet but purchasing your seat in advance usually provides a better seat.

o Where there are no deterrents there will be aggression.

o A vote can make it legal but legal cannot make it right.

o The man that shows support for that which isn't right is just as wrong.

o As the decoy manipulates the fowl, so does a foul manipulate those decoys.

o The rules are only as those whom in power dictate.

o Achievement in this world is often viewed as the one who does the jobs of many; in the next life, achievement will be seen as the one who did his own job.

o There is no such law as a permanent law.

o God does because it is right, not right because he is God.

o If they are differences, there will always be prejudices.

o So long as there is a get out of jail free card monopoly will always be played.

o A nation not being led by the bible is being pulled by it.

o When any political party becomes more important than principle it will have lost its purpose.

o Rights should extend also to those who do behave, not merely to those who do not.

o Equality is to be conditional to behavior.

o Common sense is often removed by abnormal subsidies.

o A sore will not be poked without a strong reaction; neither will the unrepentant remain kindly silent when justly charged.

o Those in authority with an evil heart that cause the truth to be deferred will not go unpunished, but those without laxity will be provided a means of escape.

o In the end, Judas always hangs himself.

o The cost of the good-guys having lots of guns is nothing compared to the bad-guys knowing that they haven't any.

o Banning guns that appear to look really mean is like banning cars because they look really fast.

o What a nation can't or refuses to recognize God will reveal one way or the other.

o Carnality doesn't change ways, just goings.

o If a democratic government can tax it the government will eventually legalize it. But the can is always left up to the will of people.

o The two best insurance policies one can own: A King-James Version bible and a personal firearm.

o The purpose of government is to restrain evil not unleash it.

o What can be hidden from daddy cannot be concealed from the father

o Laying out cheese on a mousetrap won't catch a bulldog, but if it did.

o Where there is no distinct final authority for the right, there can be no true civil governing for the wrong.

o Right is defined by God's commandments not by man's privileges.

o No good deed goes unrewarded and no bad intent goes unpunished.

o If there was more proper punishment, we would have less improper crime.

o There is no hiding blame where choice has been made obvious.

o Discipline is to be present and behavior is not to be excused.

o Being politically correct ensures being biblically inaccurate.

o Every position that is in opposition to God's position is in the wrong position.

o Man is either obeying the truth or denying it, but he is not escaping it.

o A sponge absorbs but is also occasionally rung out. So is the man who takes advantage of advantage.

o Quicker judgments produce fewer crimes.

o If behavior doesn't have a right to be scrutinized in hiring, how can it be discriminated against in firing?

o The one who elects their own course should take his own test.

o A share that isn't equally balanced is not by any means fair.

o The one who is constantly exercising excuses is rarely strengthening their answers.

o Where there is an absence of responsibility there will be a presence of turmoil.

o Running the risk of getting caught is encouraged by a slow response in executing penalty.

o Evil is prolonged where its execution is delayed.

o Where judgement is delayed remorse isn't hurried.

o Much is not to be confused with more, and little is not to be confused with less. For if more was required from much, less would be required from little.

o Loyalty is to be greatly valued, but disloyalty is not to be overpriced.

o Above every difference in practice should be the agreement in principle.

o A flat tax will put a lot of air into a deflated economy.

o A flat tax doesn't reward or penalize, it balances.

o Giving the people what they want will put one in office, having the people then pay for it will then cause his exit.

o Equality demands the same opportunity, not the same successes.

o The winner isn't always the one that is chosen.

o A conscious can be seared but the consequences cannot be severed.

o The only power of this world comes from that in which we feed it.

o Being penalized for prospering is preposterous.

o The man who tries to hide his hate with deceit from anyone will no doubt be exposed by his own hand and that to everyone.

o Fairness equates equal opportunity, not the same results.

o All of man desires equal rights, until those same rights leave us unequal.

o The one that stands opposed to the light will always cast shadows.

o The politics of candidacy can often tear down more than its election of office could ever build up.

o Man is usually taken by the excuse he generally gives.

o The pulse of a government only expresses the heart of its people.

o Where no self-control is found administered restraints should be required.

o Where there are no self-restraints there must be a governing control.

o The guilty may seek for mercy but it is the fool who attempts to escape justice.

o Setting out to get somebody generally ends up in being got by somebody.

o Mixing doesn't combine; it merely dilutes the space in which it fills.

- Gun control is best enforced by beating the criminal to the draw.
- Whenever one has begun to work against you, a salary for their efforts will have been noted and payment of return is sure to be forthcoming.
- The reactions from others should be assumed contingent according to one's own actions.
- A lack of evidence doesn't prove a lack of guilt.
- Anything not straight is crooked.
- No prison confines more men than the bars of the human mind.
- Where there is no fear of judgment there can be no appreciation for pardon.
- Hurt hurled returns.
- No confinement can release a man of his sentence
- The one prison that man cannot break is confined within' the walls of his mind.
- A bill that perpetrates hate against the righteous is criminal.
- Lightness of wrong without correction only increases the load.
- Sooner or later the match is going to strike some powder.
- Evil never quits, but good always wins.

#13

Kindness (Selfishness)

The merciful man doeth good to his own soul: but [he that is] cruel troubleth his own flesh.

Proverbs 11:17 KJV

o Sew, don't hoe.

o Gratefulness is the acknowledgment, not the expressiveness.

o Concern doesn't seek attention, but attention will seek concern.

o Courtesy cost nothing yet can buy you a lot.

o Encouragement is a powerful tool that man should be given to those who are found working with struggles.

o Mercy should be balanced but never tilted.

o Compassion is to be motivated by the heart not the government.

o The cheapest investment that will produce the greatest yield is always kindness.

o You only make yourself miserable by not being hospitable.

o Sympathize with those whose cup is half empty but rejoice because your own is half full.

o Invitations should never be sent out for a pity party.

o The greatest need of man is to be a better supplier of wants to others.

o Truth has no apologies, but its delivery is to be considered.

o Strength without gentleness is a weakness.

o Liberals often deal in feelings without thought; Conservatives often deal in thought without feelings. But the Gospel calls for all to consider them both, and that without fail.

o *Individuals shouldn't be mishandled but wrong* life-styles should be pointed out.

o Individuals are not to be shamed but their sinful life-styles are to be shunned.

o An empty life is filled with living for self.

o Man cannot destroy his enemy by hating him. But he can destroy himself by hating his enemy.

o The only person that man is sure to destroy with bitterness is himself.

o Bitterness is never the answer, it only sours the condition.

o Taking advantage of someone's wrong doesn't make it right.

o When you stop acting like someone owes you, they will more enjoy paying you.

o Respect for other expressions is often contingent on those other's expressions being respectful.

o Being beautiful is by chance, being ugly is by choice.

o Win your foes and you win the war.

o Self-control and gentleness arrest the strongest resistance.

o A lot of strength is found in a little hug.

o One is more likely to invest in you only after you have first invested in them.

o Allowing one to become comfortable is only done by making them feel welcome.

o You can measure the amount of one's praise by their own number of given compliments.

o Outcome is determined by input or the lack thereof.

o A man can work on his ways but only play on his personality.

o Ambition over exercised becomes ammunition that generally self-explodes.

#14

Knowledge (Ignorance)

The heart of the prudent getteth knowledge;
and the ear of the wise seeketh knowledge.

Proverbs 18:15 KJV

o Maturity cannot be taught, it must be lived out.

o The one paying more attention will own less embarrassment.

o It's not enough to know the truth, one must understand the truth.

o Maturity can come at a completely different place without ever leaving the same location.

o Ignorance can travel the world over and yet never arrive at the nearest truth.

o Man is only a threat to others when he begins to think for himself.

o Mellow is not to be mistaken for yellow.

o The one who doesn't learn any better cannot do any better.

o Nervousness and anxiousness look a lot alike but shouldn't ever be confused.

o The bible doesn't tell man what is right and or wrong, the bible affirms to man what is right and or wrong.

o Some will never want what you desire to give; others will desire to give that which you would never want. All should accept the truth of them both.

o The narrative is pushed only to forward an agenda: Get educated, not schooled.

o Where there is no fear of God there will be no concern for life.

o Emotions and excitement can get one into as much trouble as it can out.

o There are those who won't receive an answer merely because they enjoy their misery too much.

o The wise man will effort himself not only in faith but also in works, not only in knowledge but also in wisdom; Thankful in kindness but not settled in ignorance, appreciative for mercy but aware of justice.

o Nothing changes perception more clearly than proof of its ignorance. Nothing secures reality more definitively than a lack of evidence against it.

o To not be informed is to be uneducated, to be willingly ignorant is just plain stupid.

o When you start with the truth, facts are just a bonus.

o The battle for affection, esteem, and glory will be won through kindness, wisdom, and strength.

o Knowing when to be quick and when to be slow will always place you right on time.

o Balance keeps man upright; Understanding keeps one from falling.

o Opportunity will come knocking, but it is only the prepared that can open the door.

o Education should be pursued while chasing godly favor.

o Debate begins understanding, understanding ends debate.

o With every loss comes gain.

o There is no equality in promoting the unqualified.

o Change is only wrong when it isn't right.

o Removing the wrapper reveals that which is on the inside.

o Man is not to be defined in the middle, nor in his beginning, but rather at his end.

o The passenger may demonstratively give accurate instruction, but it is the driver that ultimately determines the direction.

o Just as a map is of no use to the blind, so is direction from the knowledgeable to the fool.

o Every given age cannot be understood until that age has been lived.

o Don't lie on the truth, take advantage of it.

o Lessons learned the hard way are more easily not forgotten.

o Some things can be taught, but most must be learned.

o A man of understanding will thirst for knowledge, and an education will feed him.

o Education should be used to broaden one's view, not to dim his perspective.

o The bible should be the center for both the left and the right.

o An education can help to provide an income, but it is wisdom that allows you to secure it.

o Where knowledge is found wisdom can be obtained.

o The wise man that finds knowledge considers self well paid.

o Once you determine the motivator there's little left to consider.

o The man that is hard to help doesn't realize the difficulty that he is causing others towards resolving his disorder.

o An issue in and of itself is not a problem. But trouble will bloom where man makes a problem out of an issue.

o Much is said in a response that is ignored, the trained ear will hear it well.

o What can't be taught can be learned, but what can't be learned can be taught.

o Innovation will progress a nation or the lack thereof will doom it.

o You can hear without listening, but you cannot listen without hearing.

o Where attention is not given retention cannot be received.

o Man should always investigate the outcome before assuming responsibility for the income.

o Advice given where it is not requested is ill-advised.

o Being sure is an uncertainty.

o Many obtain information, but few retain knowledge.

o You can't gain experience through knowledge, but you can gain knowledge through experience.

o Experience is not needed for knowledge.

o Good instructions can come from a bad instructor.

o You can often gauge the level of convictions of a man by his response once poked.

o Attention always precedes retention.

o A man's education is not limited to his schooling.

o Sin has its pull on all of man, so let us pray for strength to refuse it or the guilt to repent from it.

o Differences dictate decision.

o A formula will always produce a conclusion, but a conclusion may not always reveal a formula.

o Always start with the conclusion so that you don't end up in confusion.

o Life isn't complicated, people are.

o Obtaining knowledge and following instruction produces wisdom that yields the right results.

o Age may not reflect temperament, but maturity will.

o The difference in making a good decision and bad one is the outcome.

o When you ask for anything, you're setting yourself up for everything.

o Education without morality is ignorance.

o Innovation sustains a society.

o The modern church is a traditional barometer of an accurate society.

o Knowledge without application is escape without deployment.

o Don't wait until the voice is gone to learn to listen.

o Decision should follow instruction, not precede it.

o The pitcher takes the credit, but it is the catcher making the call.

o The life recorded last forever.

o Ignorance knows it all.

o Just because one doesn't travel doesn't mean that he doesn't know the directions.

o Knowledge is more important than strength.

o An education makes a smart man not a diploma.

o A lack of understanding promotes an abundance of speculation.

o Knowledge without wisdom is life without growth.

o The smart man doesn't dwell on what he's learned but studies on what he hasn't.

o While a solution can remove a present problem wisdom can prevent a future problem.

o One should dwell more on what he's learned through his mistakes and less on the mistakes that he's made through learning.

o Instincts bow at what is larger, insights bow at what is lower.

o There is a way which seems wrong unto a man, but the beginning thereof is the ways of life.

o An education is life's lessons learned.

o The man given a chance has no excuses.

o An unbalanced scale will tilt; so will the man who is too weighty on any one given thing.

o Balance centers everything.

o As the lips begin to crack without moisture so does man's fate without instruction.

o Trying to convey common sense to the insensible is like squeezing a rock trying to draw water.

o The person in greater need of help is the one who doesn't realize that they need it.

o Intelligence can limit man's understanding, but his spirit can reveal a multitude of discernment.

o To know a thing is smart, to learn from it is intelligence.

o Life's greatest teacher is experience.

o The best way to preserve your thoughts is to write them down.

o Life cannot be taught but it must be learned.

o   Many who claim to be woke are just sleep-walking.

15

Leadership
(Incompetence)

Let no man despise thy youth; but be thou an example of the believers, in word, in conversation, in charity, in spirit, in faith, in purity.

1st Timothy 4:12 KJV

o Leadership without a voice isn't suaveness, its cowardice.

o Youth is only for a short while, but immaturity can be found in the oldest of men.

o The preacher who is not stirred becomes stagnate.

o If you can't handle criticism don't give directions.

o Leadership's job is not to point fingers of blame, but rather to claw exoneration through results.

o Being qualified doesn't make one certified.

o Ability and authority are limited to opportunity and endorsement.

o Without wisdom man cannot make sure decisions. Where it is in use man cannot fail.

o A platform gives you the ability to leap but it also provides the means to a fall.

o Being in the spotlight will always cast a shadow.

o The pack can run no harder than its lead.

o The only requirement to lead is to stay a step ahead.

o Do not vote for the man who can do the most for you, but rather vote for the man who can be used the most by God.

o If one cannot stand up for their leader, they have no right to sit down with him.

o When the job is not getting done, the people are not doing the work.

o If you will take the pitchers best pitch away, you stand a better chance of getting on base.

o In order to be seen you first must be noticed.

o Knowledge is information; wisdom is the sense to use it.

o Win the people and you can end the war.

o Momentum is more powerful than force.

o If you step up, be prepared to get knocked down.

o If you are a leader, lead.

o Having soap with no running water is like having a church with no fiery preacher.

o Everything is only as good as its ingredients.

o A Preacher is only as good as his last sermon.

o When you allow anything, you should expect everything.

o The only way to prepare is to plan.

o The man who develops a pattern will become branded as does cattle, though his work be good or bad.

o Once cattle have become branded it is virtually impossible for them to be changed.

o Motivation is better stirred through challenge not consequences.

o With great power come great responsibilities.

o The ripple is only as strong as the splash.

o The old man doesn't want to change, and the young man doesn't want to stay the same.

o Everybody needs to answer to somebody.

o Influence is stronger than might.

o Strength is found in will not want.

o A strong man will not focus on his strength but will work on his weaknesses.

- One cannot take a position without experiencing opposition.
- The pulpit is the only place that the preacher can say to the masses what he cannot say to the individual.
- When we fail to prepare, we will have prepared to fail.
- Dwelling on the regrets of the past will only leave sorrow over the missed opportunities for the future.
- Influence weakens helplessness.
- The one making the loudest noise also creates the biggest commotion.
- Anytime you do anything, be prepared to be criticized by everyone and for everything.
- There is a vast difference in leading because one is out front, from one being out front because he wants to lead.
- The best way to protect is to prevent.
- The only way to get one to follow is to lead.
- Being at ease promotes future pains.
- It is more foolish to ask a question that knowingly has no answer than to answer the fool which poses that very question.
- The one who chases alcohol flees responsibility.
- As sure as the summer months bring expansion and the winter cold delivers contraction so will man's favor or lack thereof among his peers.
- There cannot be organization without rules.
- What is produced by one is reproduced by others.
- When you give up the floor, be prepared to watch the ceiling cave in.

o If you are not holding yourself up, you are letting others down.

o Legacy is defined on how one reacts to a crisis.

o Taking responsibility includes accepting consequences.

o Respect demands the honoring of authority.

o While under-tightening may lead to separation, over-tightening will ensure separation.

o Under-tightening may cause a leak, but over-tightening will cause a burst.

o Those whom are continually tearing down cannot build up.

o Where there are kids at play, an adult is needed to walk in the room.

16

Love (Hate)

And now abideth faith, hope, charity, these three; but the greatest of these [is] charity.

1st Corinthians 13:13 KJV

o Love's value should not be determined by its measure of expression, but expression should be measured where there is love.

o Hate isn't a color it is an evil.

o Jealousies can kill advancement, but love will resurrect the dead.

o The man who says he is willing to die for those whom he says he loves, should be able to live for them.

o Bad people look for any good excuse to do wrong.

o Give to that in which you got, as you once gave to that in which you sought.

o Love will tell a man the truth though he may not enjoy hearing it. Truth will reveal the answer though that man might not enjoy finding it.

o Love is summed up best in one word, commitment. Staying committed is determined best by one word, choice.

o It's not cupid that determines one's valentine, but it is stupid that generally loses heart.

o Whatever you love will cost you, whatever you despise will cost those whom you love.

o Being in love is not a chore, it is a deliberate decision. To stay in love is to never change your mind.

o God's gift to man is his love for him. Man's gift to God is his love for others.

o Love is not possessed where it isn't expressed.

o Care is conveyed best by truth not by comfort.

o Live for those who love you, die for those whom you love.

o Belief is made obvious by behavior.

o Whatever you love will cost you, whatever you despise will cost those whom you love.

o If you want to restore that love that you once had, give that love that you once gave.

o What love covers hatred often reveals.

o Good's greater accomplishment shouldn't be to rid the one from the evil, but to rid evil from the one.

o Love should only follow truth, and truth should never lead without love.

o There is no breech in good manners in that which is done out of sincere love.

o The depth of one's love can often be measured by the height of one's love.

o Love dissolves what hate has constructed.

o The person who always chooses to be ugly can never look good.

o True love is built on acceptance of who one is, not what one does.

o The greater appreciation will be seen not merely heard.

o A hate for sin is not to be considered a hate crime, the condoning of sin should be.

o Love without justice is criminal.

o Where love is served justice will be ordered.

o Love is the tape that holds all good things together and without which there can be no adhesive.

o Love soothes sores.

o When one cannot be pulled away it's because they are too attached.

o If love is the greatest word, then hate is the worst.

o Love covers a multitude of sins because sin covers a multitude of people.

o It is better to have lost love than to have never found it.

o It is better to have suffered loss than to have never experienced gain.

o The good memories are worth the bad losses.

o Whatever is on the inside will eventually be seen on the outside.

o It's often easier to change ones want than to break ones will.

o The only real storybook ending comes through God's Word.

o Treatment should be used to ease pain, not cause it.

o Love is birthed, nurtured and kept by decision and not by fate.

o The appreciation for one's worth most often follows at the cost of their absence.

o Love is only present where singleness is absent.

o Win your adversary and you win the war.

o Love is not blind it's just shaded.

o To love without expression is to live without purpose.

17

Marriage (Divorce)

[Whoso] findeth a wife findeth a good [thing], and obtaineth favour of the LORD.

Proverbs 18:22 KJV

o The life of the married man will reflect that of a committed relationship not merely an occasional date night.

o Marriage is a wonderful thing, to those who have such a thing.

o The antidote for poverty begins with marriage.

o The couple who works as hard to keep a marriage together as they do at putting it together will never part.

o The sole purpose of marriage is propagation.

o A lasting marriage is spent on a short memory.

o Sinlessness doesn't mess up a marriage, sinfulness does.

o The husband that no longer opens the door for his wife still loves her, he has only become more secure in their relationship.

o If each spouse will place the other ahead of themselves no one will come up short.

o The strongest influence in a man's life is a man's wife.

o By keeping your marriage fresh, it won't become stale.

o You cannot buy your marriage, but you can certainly give it away.

o Little tires a man while energizing a woman more, than a trip to the mall.

o It is the woman who can have a closet full of clothes and shoes and yet still have nothing to wear.

o As the bread goes stale that loses its freshness, so does the relationship that loses its spark.

o The only way for a couple to prevent having something to come between them is to stay close together.

o Alcohol abuse is to the marriage what Red Devil lye misuse is to your drainpipe.

#18

Money (Debt)

Wealth [gotten] by vanity shall be diminished: but he that gathereth by labour shall increase.

Proverbs 13:11

o Prosperity doesn't demand theft, but covetousness will always pursue it.

o Favors are expensive.

o A dollar shouldn't ever override one's word, and never cost one a friendship.

o Both abundance and or the lack thereof, harm countless.

o Care is to be freely given, not governmental stolen.

o A few more dollars often cost a much greater expense.

o With capitalism not everybody will be saved, but through socialism nobody can escape.

o The face of equality is often merely a mask for the envious.

o Wages doesn't determine worth, value does.

o Where money is involved and desperation is in play, foolishness will often be found at work.

o The mirror offers reflection, reflection demands truth.

o Debt is never a problem, until you're required to pay.

o Punishing success is not biblical its covetousness.

o When the rich man can no longer make a profit, then the poor man can no longer find a job.

o Stealing from one to give to another is still theft.

o Equal pay should be distributed for equal production, not for equal time.

o Debt doesn't make one a failure, not having a plan to repay will.

o There's more to be concerned with what is being done with one's own money than what another is doing with theirs.

o A financial safety net should not be used as a hammock of leisure.

o One having a tough time making payments is also causing a hard time for those to whom it is due.

o When man can no longer achieve the standard of his way of living, that value will be reset, or totally lost.

o A dollar is worth only what others value it to be.

o The one down on his luck is generally just not up on his planning.

o Overtaxing the wealthy leads to the underpaying of the poor.

o Debt is not a problem, until you can't pay for it.

o The enjoyment that we find in the things of this life is truly not found in obtaining them, but rather in being able to afford them.

o Foolishness of the rich is applauded while wisdom from the poor is ignored.

o One may enjoy spending all but will surely regret having spent all.

o More hand-outs and greater deficits will not deliver man from his financial struggles; rather it will prolong his escape.

o It is better to be broke and straight, than rich and crooked.

o Money can buy you anything in life yet nothing in death.

o Robbing from the rich is as wrong as taking from the poor.

o It's not a red or blue thing. Nor is it a white or black thing. Most often it's really about the green thing, causing it all to become a grey thing.

o Nobody likes to change but everyone enjoys advancement.

o The safest bet that you will ever make is not to gamble.

o Often the cause for insomnia comes from both the accumulation of great riches and or the lack thereof.

o The influence of cash often produces change.

o The one who does what no one else can do secures his employment.

o The man who does what nobody else desires to do secures his employment.

o Gain through wrong is loss.

o No profit should be expected where there has been no investment.

o Through justice much is gained, through bribery all is lost.

o It is better to leave a good name than to take a bad profit.

o Prosperity is lost where entitlement is gained.

o You can lose faster than you can gain.

#19

Obedience
(Disobedience)

Then Peter and the [other] apostles answered and said, We ought to obey God rather than men.

Acts 5:29 KJV

- o One of these three can always be found among disobedience in the church: Ignorance, Incompetence, and or Defiance.
- o Removing accountability of not following God's laws assures a society it will not be following man's laws.
- o Everybody can make a mistake, but nobody must continue with it.
- o A little bad can spoil a lot of good.
- o Good behavior prompts response, bad behavior accelerates it.
- o Doing right lessens the possibilities of being done wrong.
- o Obedience is always the sweetest road of travel.
- o It's better to have reservations and it restrict, than to have no doubt and live unrestrained.
- o We shouldn't obey just to be rewarded but we should be rewarded in just obeying.
- o If one is at attention, he should do his job, if it's not his job he shouldn't be an attention.
- o We are not all called to minister the same, but we're all the same called to minister.
- o The choice is always men; the outcome is always God's.
- o Success is seeking to please God; however one's career turns out.
- o Behavior is birthed from belief.
- o God generally deals with man in private before he chastens him in public.
- o It's better to listen to God while he's in your ear, and not others.

o Motivation doesn't give permission to its execution.

o It's little because people don't believe, and mostly because they won't commit.

o Everyone desires to completely escape hell, but few want to totally surrender to Christ.

o God isn't against the government that is for him, but God is against the government who sides against him.

o Everybody seems to be a Christian, but nobody tends to be a Saint.

o It is in error to seek God's blessings before seeking God's approval.

o Yielding comes before stopping, as does consideration before decision.

o Where there is more obedience there will be less offense.

o Doing good is a lot of work, but the benefits far exceeds one's labors.

o Where rules are not long followed on the job, the job won't long be followed by the one.

o One incident can affect a lifetime of achievements.

o The best way to be prepared is not to slow down, but rather to fast.

o Man often struggles with deliverance needlessly because he has struggled in prayer and fasting unfaithfully.

o Obedience to the general thing will lead you to the recognition of the specific thing.

o A sermon is only as good for you as it is applied by you.

o Experience escapes a many of danger, but the youth will seldom go without punishment.

o Where God's commandments are being followed man's laws will be pursued.

o Don't pick the scripture that fits, fit the scriptures that you pick.

o Doing right will keep you away from a lot of wrong.

o The weights of life can often be avoided by simply not overloading the cart.

o The thin thread of sin left unbroken will lead to a rope that easily cannot.

o Drunkenness always has a hangover, and so does all sin its miseries.

o The one who stirs will be settled.

o Appreciation should stand with one's denomination, but loyalty should lay with the Lord.

o Holiness is the cure to sinfulness.

o When one's view becomes dim his vision will become strained.

o Loss of spiritual sight comes from the gain of worldly view.

o The one who refuses to mind cannot learn.

o One's past is always before him.

o The way of the rebellious is down-hill.

o True thanksgiving to God is being obedient.

o The best way to get a child to straighten up is to bend him over.

o God's goodness is not dependent upon his performance, but his performance is dependent on our
  goodness.

o Mercy should always follow justice and not precede
  it. For if there be any mercy before justice then there
  isn't any fairness.

o As a society becomes more liberal, the bible becomes
  more offensive.

o Gravity and judgement are inescapable and inevitable to all.

o The way to keep the outward man from getting dirty
  is by keeping the inward man clean.

o Scriptures consumed works as a medicine, things
  get better.

o Walking on the edge will cause one to lose his balance.

o One slip often removes all ground gained; so can one
  mistake erase a lot of good.

o Nobody enjoys discipline, but everyone loves its
  benefits.

o To the obedient God is love and mercy, but to the
  defiant he is fear and dread.

o Most people can see when the anointing comes, and
  know when it's there, but few can see when it leaves.

o Strength is always found in a wise man, but wisdom
  is not always found in a strong man.

o A good word coming from a bad mouth is like clean
  water offered from a dirty glass.

o Man fails by one of only three things; either what
  looks good, feels good or that which is his arrogance.

o Preaching God's word is often like throwing darts in the dark. You don't know exactly where they are going, but you know that something or someone is getting the point.

o The assumption of a thing often follows the history of a thing.

o One's past always follows his future.

o The greatest shame of a parent is most often the disobedience of his child.

o An unstable man is like the waves of the sea. Up and down in and out and absolutely cannot be trusted.

o In order to get God to work for you, you must first work for him.

o God is obligated to those who are obligated to him.

o What you put before you will always follow you.

o The freedom to choose restricts the ability to blame.

o Making our own decisions constructs our own outcome.

o Where there is no penalty neither can there be reward.

o Accountability is birthed from the death of responsibility.

o It's man's nature to do wrong, yet it is his duty to do right.

o A hurricane's position can be pin pointed, but its path cannot be predicted; so it is with the man who stirs the anger of God.

o One cannot be threatened of loss that has nothing to lose.

o There is no control present where there is an absence of consequences.

- To not know the truth and to continue is ignorance; To know the truth and persist is stupidity.
- The eaglet that no longer finds comfort in the nest should find its own roost, as should the child who troubles his own parents.
- Ones actions prompts others words.
- Satan believes in God, but it is the Christian that follows God.
- Sin will take you to new heights in old lows.
- Everyone has something to lose and everyone something to gain.
- As the itch demands a scratch, so do man's actions require justice.
- Man should not be condemned for his sins, but his sins neither should go without being condemned.
- The man who will not listen to reason cannot comply to judgment.
- Commanding a fool to use good judgment is like requesting a dog not to bark.
- God's favor follows greatly those who follow him closely.
- Don't wait until you can't to decide that you will.
- A law in only as good as its enforcement.
- To place a blessing on what God has already damned is a curse.
- The follower without obedience is like a leader without direction.
- To follow right is to not lean towards the left.
- The right view will keep you from going left.

o To not go right is to go liberal; to not go left is to go right.

o By not minding the present we will resent the future.

o Where there's an absence of guidelines there will be a presence of chaos.

o Though few appreciate restrictions, many benefits from its value.

o The man that is confident of the favor of God has no fear of the anger of men.

o Man's actions produce either rewards or consequences.

o Embarrassment soon follows the child that often wanders.

o Doing right cost now: Doing wrong cost later.

o If you will stay in tune you won't lose your rhythm.

o To honor duty where there is no delight is a delightful duty.

o The only way to stay out of the dark is to remain in the light.

o Behavior provokes response.

#20

Patience (Restlessness)

And let us not be weary in well doing: for in due season we shall reap, if we faint not.

Galatians 6:9 KJV

o When you're not sure of your steps, you slow your pace.

o Don't be too quick to get on the bus, know where it is going.

o Restraint will be the hardest thing one will ever do.

o Pressure is no excuse to blow; deflate.

o You don't have to be doing anything wrong, God may just be wanting to do something right.

o The greater testimony may be to be sustained in your suffering not delivered from it.

o If a man cannot see colors, encourage him to work to distinguish the shades. For a little inspiration has allowed even the blind to reveal to others, much.

o If both the circle and the square are made, then they both indeed can be reshaped.

o Response reveals regard.

o Affect effects.

o Where the need calls for it, a nail shouldn't be merely tapped but rather greatly walloped.

o Balance keeps one from falling not strength.

o If you will continue to push something will eventually begin to move.

o Bells and whistles often make more than enough noise.

o There is no way to sling mud without getting dirty.

o Moving forward doesn't assure the right direction.

o First instinct is usually right, first reaction usually isn't.

o When we are out of place nothing quite fits.

- The clever mind will be exposed by the hidden heart.
- The weight of stress is no reason to unload.
- Trouble doesn't assure failure, only struggle.
- One's appearance is improved significantly by hiding others ugliness repeatedly.
- Doing right can cost now, but a full re-imbursement will come later, with benefits.
- Nothing reveals more than time.
- You don't turn the water off because it is cold; you wait for it to warm up.
- Strength tires, but stamina endures.
- Where failure is never present success is always absent.
- When you know that you don't have as much powder, make certain that you have the shortest fuse.
- Meekness is not a weakness but rather strength.
- A fool's temper can cause damage to others, but self-destruction is assured for himself.
- There's no need in looking for your specific purpose until you've fulfilled your basic training.
- Side effects can be worse than the problem.
- Deep thoughts prevent shallow actions.
- Tomorrow always comes, but it takes twenty-four hours.
- It's ok to knock, but being invited will more likely make you welcomed to come in.
- One way to keep from getting dirty is to simply wait for the dust to settle.

- If you're going to have anything you have go to put up with everything.
- Desires are sweetened even more by extended waits.
- The gambler's gain creates loss.
- A wall doesn't just appear; it is built.
- A lack of speed won't slow the persistent down.
- Failure is only an opportunity for another start.
- One bump in the road isn't worth avoiding the entire trip.
- Words are only as strong as the power we give to them.
- One way to help avoid getting dirty is to wait for the dust to settle.
- Every man should have his rights along with the intelligence to reserve them.
- In order to have a beginning and an end; you must also have a middle.
- Before one can get to the top he must first begin with a climb.
- A Pharaoh is often placed behind us only to then move us towards yet a red sea.
- The difference in those who are successful and those who are not, some just keep going and others do not.
- Where one won't, many will.
- When one cuts corners they merely go around in circles.
- A surfer cannot be considered great until he has first faced the waves.

o Our outcome is not determined by our circumstances, but rather our reactions to our circumstances.

o Going backwards is often one's best move forward.

o Through the adversity of nature comes the diversity of man.

o Longsuffering is often prompted by one's quick temperament.

o Capturing the moment last forever.

o A Recording never ages.

o To council with a fool is like reasoning with a drunk.

o For every positive there's always a negative.

o A slow retreat is often the result from a quick response.

o Patience is wiser than passion.

o The warmth of summer is as certain as the cold of winter.

o Nothing helps a long-winded preacher shorten his sermons like after having sat and heard another long-winded preacher.

o Patience prolonged is stressed.

o Focus provides clarity while neglect causes blindness.

o Strong Christians don't have fewer problems than others; they've just trained themselves to better handle the weight.

o The man who looks for fault will find it.

o Friction creates heat as does the man that overstays his welcome.

o The one that is most visible is often the last one to be seen.

o Thrill seekers stick around only until the next big show comes to town.

o The surest way to get along with others is to spend time alone with one's self.

o The man who is no longer getting into a thing is on his way of getting out of it.

o An education must not merely be taught but also learned.

o The man that exercises restraint will rest from arousal.

o With every advance comes a setback.

o If discipline runs ones off chaos will bring them back.

o Those who are barely planted can hardly be fruitful.

o There can be no evil raised that goodness cannot bring down.

o Time should allow the Christian to rethink not regroup.

o God speaks to man in private before he exposes him to the public.

o Nothing inspires noise more than silence.

o It's often good to see visitors come but it's always great to see them go.

o Work hard when no one is watching and your rewards will come when everyone is looking.

o Nothing reveals more than time, nothing.

o Stress simply carries the blame for the weight that we often unload.

o For if when we are young, we can handle the stresses of failure then as we grow older, we can better control the reactions of our successes.

#21

Peace (Struggle)

If it be possible, as much as lieth in you, live peaceably with all men.

Romans 12:18 KJV

o Where truth has been rejected, division is certain to be adopted.

o With those whom with there can be no peace, don't be ugly, don't be spiteful, just be done.

o If you're going to give it to them, you better be prepared to take it from them.

o It's better to put distance between those whom you can't get along than closeness.

o The young man seeks for ways to get in, and the old man looks for ways to get around.

o Some keep it settled, and some just keep it stirred.

o Dissention causes restriction.

o Some have it better than everybody else, some have it worse than everybody else, but both choose how they decide to have it and nobody else.

o Being principled will keep one from having to make a lot of decisions.

o Jesus didn't hang Peter, pastors shouldn't either.

o Decide today and there will be no question tomorrow.

o Enjoy today, tomorrow will come: When tomorrow arrives look forward to today.

o Man can only feel what he is sensitive to, that's why God rubs him with it.

o God gives much, few discover it.

o One sure way to avoid contention is not to take part in it.

o The one who will work on the why instead of the what, can rest in the now instead of the later.

o To reach an answer to prayer we must grasp the will of God.

o The devil keeps busy, but God stays in control.

o Being at peace shouldn't come at the expense of giving the enemy time to reload.

o Every people at war desire a man of peace; every people at peace requires a man of war.

o Man is to change for the better, but not worse for the sake of change.

o Man shouldn't spend his life trying to get there at the expense of being miserable if he doesn't.

o One can flee from the truth, but it will follow him everywhere he goes.

o Diplomacy is to be given the price of chance but not at the cost of bankruptcy.

o There is no excuse for wrong, and there is no remorse for truth.

o No matter how close you follow you will always lag.

o Strength is the only sure means of weakening those who seek to rob it.

o Trouble may be found but refuge should be sought.

o Need is met through God's supply for the man who will only accept it.

o Those whom are not in harmony will always take the group out of key.

o The death penalty doesn't promote killing, it condemns murder. So does a weapon in the hand of the innocent deter the would be guilty.

o You can't prevent evil but you dead sure can stop it.

o Gun ownership doesn't incite lawlessness it prevents it.

o Excitement or serenity; neither satisfies.

- Everyone seeks for peace but few settles for it.
- Spiritual strength comes from fleshly restraint not its overindulgence.
- There can be no position taken where there won't be opposition given.
- Strive to be at peace where you can; but prepare for war where you cannot.
- Failure's biggest target is success.
- Fires die down if they are not continually stirred up.
- It's not important where it went wrong, only that you've made it right.
- Only God can comfort the soul that battles the flesh.
- Strength to face the bad news is found in the reading of the good news.
- It is better to be blessed in poverty than to be cursed in prosperity.
- Happiness is contingent on thigs of this world, while peace is only available through things not of this world.
- One cannot savor peace without having tasted turmoil.
- Hiding leaves room for much to be uncovered while coming clean frees the dirt.
- Man can escape what's before his eyes but not what's between his ears.
- Calm comes behind the storm not in front of it.
- Satisfaction is found only in being satisfied.
- The one who stirs perplexity spills his integrity.
- Whatever a man chews on will bite him.

o One must fight during war time and prepare for it during the peace

o When you joy in your job, your job will become a joy.

o Disharmony destroys dynasties.

o Strive to be at peace where possible but prepare for war where it is not.

> o Not wanting anything brings a peace to everything.

o Inner peace is the result of not taking offense to being outwardly offended

o You can't stop people from offending you, but you can stop being offending by people.

o Tension leads to dissension, dissension leads to disharmony, and disharmony then in turn leads to destruction.

o Trouble produces more work, while work produces less trouble.

o True wisdom is to believe in God and doubt in self.

o To be at peace with one's self, he must first be at peace with his enemy.

o For one to be completely rounded, he must first be completely whole.

o Terrorism is one enemy that can bring every nation together.

o The computer can be deleted of its files, but the programmer will remember its content.

o Converting to truth doesn't bring shame, but rather relief.

o Jealousy prompts criticism.

o Peace is often found only through war.

- Division multiplies subtractions before there can be any additions.
- You will not worry unless you will to worry.
- Exposing division reveals unity.
- Fault can always be found where it is sought.
- The one who doesn't contribute to the commotion cannot be a part of the disturbance.
- Adding division multiplies subtraction.
- The one thing man seeks for most on the outside can only be found on the inside.
- To know relief is not to live pain free but rather to be freed from the pain from which you once lived.
- Medicines forecast relief from pain, but they also bring showers of disorder to the mind.
- Though medicines tend to ease the pain they can also worsen man's condition.
- The man who does not stand for what is right only settles for what's left.
- To argue with the un-peaceable is to kick against the dust. You don't remove it you only stir it up.
- One voice is a complaint; multiple complainers are a problem.
- A guilty conscience demands a remorseful repentance.
- Cursed are the troublemakers.
- Changing the outside may not always change what's on the inside but changing the inside will always change what's on the outside.
- When we can fix our mind on God, we will break our thoughts on self.

o When one dwells on the bad, he ignores all that is good.

o Do you really want to get in front of someone who can't get out of their own way?

#22

Pride (Humility)

[When] pride cometh, then cometh shame:
but with the lowly [is] wisdom.

Proverbs 11:2 KJV

o   None should be shining another's shoe, but all should be washing one another's feet.

o   When a man has trouble getting out of his own way, somebody else will usually come along and help him.

o   Doubling down multiplies up.

o   The humble will fight a host of lies, but it is the proud that will likely be taken by a single truth.

o   The length that the proud will go to deny truth is immeasurable.

o   The proud man doesn't believe he needs the work of the cross, he believes his works entitle him.

o   When the rebellious can't win the battle of one truth, he simply shifts to deny another one.

o   Don't wait till the end to settle, because you never know when the settle will end. End it and be settled.

o   It wouldn't be as hard on self, if self wasn't as hard on others.

o   Your not working on you is likely working on someone else.

o   The one not working on self is likely working on others.

o   Truth ignored is rebellion chosen.

o   Sanctification is a work; salvation is a decision.

o   The proud man will hide from the truth, deny the truth, and then lie about the truth.

o   The lost man can think that he is saved because he always behaves, but the saved man can know that he saved though he doesn't behave always.

o   Pride never looks in the mirror, only out the window.

o   Truth will not change the man who refuses it, his pride will continue him in his way.

o The humble never enjoys embarrassment, but it is the proud that will always deny embarrassment.

o Haughtiness comes before humiliation, but honor follows the humble.

o Pride doesn't let up; it only digs a little deeper.

o Some just want to be right; others just don't want to be wrong.

o Pride drowns the man that refuses to dip into the pool of truth.

o People will forgive you for having been wrong, but not so much when you're right.

o Talent without anointing is but a noise, regardless of how well it's played.

o Where man can't be motivated by praise, he might be by embarrassment.

o Humiliation sparks accusations of insinuations; the wise will seek to correct it; the unwise will then look to deflect it.

o Believing in somebody else and empowering them may be the greatest accomplishment of one's life.

o A player doesn't make a play the team does.

o Emotions should follow convictions not Trump them.

o That in which one prides himself will let him down.

o If you will guard what goes in, you won't be ashamed of what comes out.

o Rain doesn't seek our permission; we are to just use enough of wisdom to get out of it.

o Every team win begins with an individual effort.

o When being yourself is someone other than God intends for you to be, its wrong.

o Nobody snaps until they have first become hard.

o It's good for the dog that he never bites the tail in which he chases, for if he could, he would most likely realize it to be that of his own.

o Man, in his arrogance always affirms his ignorance.

o The humble see themselves as bearing a cross, the proud however view themselves as wearing a crown.

o No man is above error, but every man should be above its excuse.

o Submission to guilt lessens the blow of its penalty, but to the one who is resistant the sentence pronounced is hard.

o Man shouldn't view himself as being holier than thou, but he should be seen by others as trying hard.

o Every strength has a weakness.

o The hardest lessons in life to learn oftentimes come from the simplest of test.

o Being wrong is not finality, not changing from it is.

o The truth is the most important thing in life, how we respond to it is the most important thing in death.

o Spread knowledge but refrain from authorship.

o There hasn't a big man been made that a little man can't lower.

o The proud man that is just being good and not doing good or just doing good and not being good isn't near as good as he boasts.

o Man doesn't have to dig to find dirt, it is right there under his feet.

o Man needs to be shaken in order to be better steadied.

- Carnal acknowledgement is man's first step towards spiritual repentance.
- Everyone has been, is, or will be, dependent on someone else.
- Tell a wise man a truth and he will humble himself to obtain it, but resentment will always rise in the heart of those who do not seek for it.
- Ruins are restored by the anguish of a praying, fasting and repentant heart.
- The man that is humble cannot be humbled.
- Nothing humbles pride as quickly as shame.
- The closed mind is often sealed by a cracked head.
- Gravity humbles everyone.
- The man that raises himself up to be seen will only later be lowered to depths that he could not have foreseen.
- When guidance is no longer desired, instruction is no longer heard, and success will be no longer achieved.
- One should so dress as if they've been washed from their sins, not as if they're preparing to be showered from their germs.
- The more man builds himself up, the more he will let himself down.
- A measure of humility helps to avoid the pains of pride.
- Righteousness is not absent of unrighteousness.
- When everyone is the problem no one can be the solution.
- To escape by abuse is enslavement.
- Right abused is wrong.

o The one that boasts spirit-filled too often tends to leak.

o Today's humility prevents tomorrow's embarrassment.

o The more one builds themselves up in their successes the greater they will let themselves down in their failures.

o Being in the spotlight often leads to blindness.

o Wisdom begins to come in when pride begins to go out.

o The man that is full of self will spill it.

o It is when people become comfortable that they begin to make others uncomfortable.

o True morality is not present where God's instructions are absent.

o The mechanic that has no need for instruction is in no shape for advancement.

o If you stick yourself up, someone else is going to knock you back down.

o Ignorance says that there is neither knowledge to be learned nor teacher to give it.

o No man can come too early to repentance, but every man can wait until it's too late.

o Every man desires the right to wrong but hates the wrong he suffers from his rights.

o When you think you've got it, you're just before getting it.

o Often simply by thinking of where one came and where they are going, it is fuel enough to continue the trip.

o One who refuses to listen cannot hear.

o When you think you've got it, that's when you've had it.

o The only time one should look down on another, is when one is bending over to help lift them up.

o It is better to be called up than to be told to sit down.

o One must know his history to be able to appreciate his past.

o It is better to learn through other's mistakes than to gain knowledge through one's own.

o From the beginning we make our own decisions, and in the end our decisions will have made us.

o The one jabbing at another shouldn't be surprised when he is then punched.

o It's the nature of ignorant to continue in their ignorance.

o The man that is selfish and proud will more likely offend others. As well will the man offended more likely be selfish and proud.

o There's a vast difference in committing a sin and condoning that sin.

o Never set the bar higher than you're willing to jump.

o Anytime you stand up for sin you are going to get slammed down by sin.

o One's view is determined by their position.

o Independents tend to lose on their Independence.

o One who desires to ultimately be right must accept being untimely proved wrong.

o The man who praises himself is despised by many.

o The surest path to being humbled is a walk with pride.

o A walk with swagger ends with a run from pride.

o Confidence will promote you, but pride will condemn you.

o Repentance of one's sins should come as often as the gathering of fallen leaves from the Magnolia tree.

o The man who stands the highest also has the longest fall.

o No man is above being lowered.

o Man's greatest strength is also often his greatest weakness.

o The secure man is most vulnerable.

o Placing one's self in the spotlight reveals a caution light to others.

o A person will never get anywhere if they've already arrived.

o More hangings are delivered by oneself than by the executioner.

o It's ok to grow, if we never get grown.

o Man is to grow but never to become grown.

o Nothing humbles man more than being humbled.

o The man that forgets his past condemns his future.

o When man becomes small in his eyes, then he becomes big in God's eyes.

o To sin without shame is foolishness. To sin without acknowledgement is hopelessness.

o A good man will have as many get ups as he does knock downs.

o With every fall the just man will get back up.

o Every man must wait on another.

o It is the foolish man that waits until he is knocked down before he realizes the need to look up.

o The one who only desires to be out front will always leave others behind.

o The man that won't change cannot be helped.

o Providing a means of escape for the fool will only lead to his recapture.

o One cannot be led that refuses to follow.

o The smart man will refrain from giving instruction to those ignorant enough not to desire it.

o Man has the choice to either bend or break, but every knee shall bow before God.

o Those who see themselves as small are viewed by God as big.

o The larger the pistol the greater the target.

o The only thing more repulsive than a big-shot displaying is a little-shot posing.

o The person that cannot get along with everybody can rarely get along with anybody.

o When you put yourself up someone else will knock you down.

o What a man prides in will often be to his own embarrassment.

#23

Purpose (Chance)

A man's heart deviseth his way: but the LORD directeth his steps.

Proverbs 16:9 KJV

o What is being pointed out often is just being redirected.

o It's inescapable; one will be in the news, carry the news, and or make the news.

o If there were no measure of time, there could be no calculation of age.

o Gender is determined by nature not by nurture.

o Every character has a script, and every script has an author.

o The only requirement to lead is to stay a step ahead.

o The warmth of summer is as certain as the cold of winter.

o Don't wait until something bad happens to get motivated, get motivated and keep something bad from happening.

o Even when you're wasting your time, you're learning something.

o The best in this life is to enjoy it while we have it, and to try and leave it a little better for someone else when we don't.

o Make time, while you have time to make.

o Don't wait till a breakdown to get fixed; be serviced, regularly.

o If it's your job do your duty, if it's not your duty find yourself a job.

o When you can't do anything make sure you're doing something.

o If you will change your thoughts, you will change how you feel.

o Momentum and leverage are greater than speed and strength.

o Everything counts–it just doesn't all add up.

o Know your role, but be preparing for the next skit.

o You're too old when you decide you're not young enough.

o The surest way to convince someone of a thing is to spend the rest of your life proving it.

o The stoplight, while red, concludes a simple decision, so does green. But yellow can be most complicated.

o It can be turned around, if one will only take a hold of it.

o When your strategy is not to have a strategy that is your strategy.

o If you are not out front, get behind something and push.

o What you can't run off, you can lead away; and what you can't catch, you can lure in.

o Response can only come from an action; control the action and you will control the response.

o It is better to be prepared in vain than to be unprepared and surprised.

o Be the one whom God desires for you to be and settle for nothing less, because there isn't anything more.

o It takes something significant to spark sincerity. It takes sincerity to light something significant.

o God more often provides through the hands of those who prepare.

o Life is sometimes questioned, but death is always certain.

o Being at drift is not where you need to be, regardless of where you tie off at.

o Greater strength is found in a tighter grip.

o To be viewed in a different light one must change the wattage of the bulb.

o Never lose hope, never find quit; but rather continue in the faith, love and obedience.

o Stress, when properly directed, can also be used as a fuel to propel one into the right direction. Don't waste what has been burdened upon you, use it.

o Alcohol may bring it out of the mouth, but something else will have first put it into the heart.

o There's only one reason as to why some do and some don't, that is that some will, and some won't.

o The tool is subject to the hand of the carpenter, so is a gun of its owner.

o It is the spark that ignites the fire, but it is the conditions that enable the spark.

o Excitement generates interest, interest generates profit, and profit generates excitement.

o Passion primarily prolongs while calmness commonly contracts.

o Where there isn't any incentive or deterrent, little will be the effort and accomplishment.

o Timing isn't everything, but it is always just seconds away.

o It is better to put on an act of what is right than to wear the truth of that which is wrong.

o One thing that every man that starts in this life is destined to see is his end.

o God uses mistakes to fix things.

o You cannot erase history, but you can re-write the future.

o If 10% can put it all in the tank, it only takes 10% to bring it all back out.

o Change is inevitable, sure as the grave.

o The worse thing about being where you're not supposed to be is not being in the place that you're supposed to be.

o A time of a major crisis is merely a moment for simple character.

o Excitement loses momentum because of rest.

o Man is warmed by the flame he fans the most.

o Getting to where one desires to be doesn't start tomorrow, but rather its pursuit begins today.

o The one who doesn't take a position has indeed taken a position.

o Poor grammar is often a means of a richer expression.

o The best thing that could ever happen to a man is usually the worst thing that could ever happen to him.

o God provides weight to strengthen man, but it's up to man to lift those weights to gain that strength.

o The best help that one often receives comes from another attempting to do them the worst harm.

o What others mean for our harm God allows for our good.

o Circumstances mold us to be what we will have become.

o It isn't what a man drives that determines his destination but rather what drives him.

o The emphasis is to be placed where the emphasis is being demanded.

o Where man has no choice, God has a purpose.

o Where the line is undefined there can be no accountability.

o Successes are found where emphasis is given.

o Action prompts reaction.

o Every sound carries a message.

o Nothing short of taking the world over would stop the evil man if it were not for the Spiritual man.

o Purpose is realized when selfish desires are lost.

o The man that chooses solely by his free will is destined to pay a huge price.

o It's only until you can see your future that you can work towards it.

o Time is either your greatest friend or your worst enemy.

o The path to perfection is an endless road that is meant to be traveled by all.

o The worse thing happening to the Christian is the best thing that could happen for the Christian.

o Change is good when needed, consistency is better where possible.

o The only way to get to where we need, is to place God first where he needs to be.

o Where there is no strategy, confusion will there be plenty.

o The principal prayer in life should be for the principal thing.

o As sure as every target has a mark, every sermon has its audience.

o When the easy is handled as if it were difficult, then the difficult can be handled as if it were easy.

o Principal is to always come before interest.

o Credit is to be appreciated but results are to be pursued.

o There's never a second time to do a thing that you did first.

o Change affects everything.

o Nature can be curbed, manipulated, and or rerouted, but it cannot be stopped.

o While fellowship is supposed to bring people together for a cause a social gathering will often tear people apart for no reason.

o Hidden position is made visible by bumping into it.

o The ability to show change comes first from seeing the need.

o Symptoms are often the alarm that prevents one from being late.

o There can be no guidance where a course has not yet been set.

o Possible blessings walk a close line to potential curses.

o Letting off steam always alarms attention.

o If man will be the spark, God will provide the fire.

o Stoning a Stephen only raises a Paul.

o Will, must be broken to change want.

o Seeing what isn't there often causes it to appear.

o Planning should begin with not getting left behind.

o Capitalization brings emphasis to the truth. So does exclamation from the preacher to God's word.

o Passion propels persistence.

o Accomplishing one's goals is not what is most important, but rather that one is doing his best to achieve them.

o History doesn't roll backwards, its unveiled moving forward.

o There can be no prophecy where there isn't any history.

o The end is only as certain as its beginning.

o An outcome can be determined where the equation is uncovered.

o There is always an answer where there is a formula.

o The three motivators of life are love, hate and or unconcern.

o Everything seen while we're asleep has meaning of something while we're awake.

o In order to see improvement, we must first view our need.

o The person who takes no aim shouldn't be surprised of no results.

o Liquid merely fills the space that it is given; So does sin invade the soul that makes room for it.

o No one can place their future into their past, but everyone can take their past out of their future.

o Momentum begins with the effort of exertion, so does wisdom come through strains of experience.

o Excitement draws interest, interest draws dividends.

o The only person that should commit to teaching is the one who cannot restrain from teaching.

o When you take pleasure in a thing you will receive pleasure out of it.

o Work ethic comes solely from determination, determination comes by choice.

o Cause shouldn't determine choice, purpose should.

o Threat provides motivation.

o When we fill ourselves with faith, hope and charity we will rid ourselves of doubt, despair and hate.

o Man is defined best by that which he is consumed most.

o If it's for you to do, you're supposed to do it.

o Stress motivates man to action.

o God doesn't allow stress to come the Christians way to weaken us, but rather to strengthen us.

o Things don't fall into place they fall into pieces. Being placed comes by design and not by chance.

o One must often be crippled before he can begin a new walk.

o Blindness must sometimes occur before man can see.

o There is no control without restraints.

o Without balance everything will be off.

o One can always quit, but one cannot always start.

o One will generally get what he expects.

o It's not how long of a time that you spent there, but it's the quality of time you spent while you were there.

- o The greater priority in one's earthly life is not his future, but rather his present.
- o The end of a thing is merely the beginning of another.
- o There's a unique ability in every disability.
- o Focusing on priorities blinds the insignificant.
- o When times grow darker ones light should glow brighter.
- o Change is found in the ticks of a clock, but its hands revert to their former setting.
- o As memory becomes worse, forgetfulness becomes forgotten.
- o The path to riches and a meaningful life are found in those who do not seek it.
- o The greatest teacher in life is life.
- o The means of delivery should always be adopted through the plans of acceptance.
- o The greatest certainty in life is change.
- o Will is stronger than might.
- o Often the best medicine for insomnia is hard work.
- o Schooling eventually comes to an end, an education doesn't.
- o What's put in first is most often the last thing out.
- o A life without purpose is all together miserable.
- o Gas and water both have their benefits; but mixed they become of no effect.
- o The cure towards financial deficit is work; the cause for it is rest.

o Alcohol makes you feel like you could take on a bear. Taking on the bear reminds you that you shouldn't drink alcohol.

o For every villain there is a victor.

o Dreams are subconscious views that are derived from the spirit of one's past, present and or future. There are no insignificant dreams.

o To interpret a dream is to illuminate the dark.

o The whore who gives of herself to advance will be taken by loss in her decline.

o One can only govern what the government allows to be governed.

o When one discontinues his climb, he begins his descent.

o When everything is going our way it's likely not all going God's way.

o Living it up most often tears something down.

o One's destination is determined by their drive.

o While history was meant to be made, the future is meant to be developed.

o Little details make up big ideas.

o A number achieved is merely a mark to be passed.

o Righteousness isn't created it is developed.

o Probability or the lack thereof, is both contingents upon chance.

o No government can survive benefits without requirements.

o Those that mask their intentions fool themselves.

- The man that hides his selfish purpose will be exposed by his own egotistical motive.
- It is impossible to get ahead without stretching your neck.
- The man that doesn't take a position will have no sense of direction.
- The same thing that turns one man toward God turns another from God.
- The man that doesn't take a position shouldn't be given of his opinion.
- Complaints shouldn't be voiced where rules have not been established.
- Criticism shouldn't be directed where awareness has been made.
- Where the opportunities for success are small the likelihood of disaster is great.
- Where much justice is being established there is need for little favor.
- The soul without purpose is all together miserable.
- Real success is only found amid God's will.
- The one who stays busy will tire of idleness.
- Good habits deter bad behavior.
- Motivation is sparked by either rewards or punishment.
- Man is not to serve Go because it feels good, but rather because it is good.
- Where there are no barriers there can be no restrictions.
- Where there are no restraints there will be indulgences.

o Life, liberty and the pursuit of happiness is birthed by death, repression and the surrender of sorrow.

o Landmarks are not to be moved but transportation will vary.

o A great accomplishment isn't necessarily limited to having personally created one; sometimes it is simply in having supported one.

#24

Sacrifice (Rescue)

To do justice and judgment [is] more acceptable to the LORD than sacrifice.

Proverbs 21:3

o There's nothing more crucial in life to protect than to protect life itself.

o Don't wait 'till when you can no longer play the devil to mean business with God.

o Those who can should; so that those who can't won't.

o Life shouldn't end at an inconvenience, at any age.

o Protection is biblical, denial is futile.

o The one who doesn't stay the course will not finish the trip.

o Man is to want to pray; for prayer teaches him what he ought to want.

o Contributions follow investments.

o When man seeks to please God, he will offend the devil.

o Every cloud that is filled will eventually pour; Consider where you store your rain.

o You can't take it with you, but you can send it on ahead.

o Heavenly rewards will not come by what man accomplishes, but rather by what he efforts him to accomplish.

o Nothing in this life is greater than one's health, but no health is greater than one's next life.

o You've only gone too far when you can no longer turn around.

o The man that truly believes the word of God to be his greatest treasure will effort himself not only to know it, and understand it, but also protect it.

o Loyalty is only second to surrender.

o Where there hasn't been any struggle there can be no appreciation for relief.

o If one's testimony doesn't cause him to have to either duck or pucker, he hasn't got much of a testimony.

o Loyalty paid without a price is worthless.

o A gift is better to be judged by its sacrifice than its value.

o Depending on the undependable is like putting eggs in a basket filled with holes.

o Inclusion demands availability.

o Whatever you attempt to run down you will always have to give chase.

o The person who doesn't desire to be tied down to commitment should first consider the one who was nailed down for their love.

o Invitations yield attendees and laborers produce a harvest; but where there is no work there will be much hunger.

o You don't cross the plate without having rounded the bases.

o What you put into it is what you generally get out of it.

o Its okay not to win; just don't lose.

o Wisdom's gain often comes through man's loss.

o Man's fall is made harder the higher he climbs.

o One doesn't have to like the heat from the temperature to enjoy the warmth that it provides.

o Anytime you stand expect to get floored.

o The only way to keep from being put on the sideline is to have never been in the game.

o To express regret for preaching truth because of offense is like asking for forgiveness from the child for disciplining him due to his crying.

o The man who doesn't spend any time shouldn't expect to receive any change.

o The cause must be taken away for the effect to come to an end.

#25

Suffering (Comfort)

Many [are] the afflictions of the righteous:
but the LORD delivereth him out of them all.

Psalms 34:19 KJV

o Life's greatest gain can come at the expense of a most painful loss.

o The best thing that could ever happen to you may be the worst thing to have ever happened to you.

o When it rains it pours, but once it has poured it shines.

o The child that becomes unruly often becomes uncomfortable.

o When something is working against you, you're only being sharpened.

o Adversity, not accomplishments, reveals heroes.

o All heroes don't win, and all winners aren't heroes.

o There is comfort to be found in weakness, for you know strength will come from it.

o The moment to shine our brightest can only come in the darkest hour.

o A light can only be found in darkness, so can a leader only be discovered in time of need.

o Good times reflect who you desire to be, tough times reveal who you truly are.

o Man's greatest gains will have come at the expense of the highest cost.

o Hardships should make one softer.

o We can't escape this life without trouble, but we can be delivered from it.

o Standing for God often causes one to have to duck.

o In order to achieve blissful success, you will have to first experience grievous failure.

o Bad experiences don't dissolve good outcomes.

o Facing today's failures directs one towards tomorrow's successes.

o Good health cannot be accurately appreciated until one has experienced its loss.

o As certain as the ash fertilize the soil, so does the wise man profit who has been burned.

o There is a blessing and a joy in every burden to those who will only seek for it.

o Where there is no struggle there can be no victory.

o A smooth highway can lure you to sleep, but a bumpy road will keep you awake.

o It's a shame to put a lot in, to only remove yourself and be left out.

o The only man who hasn't seen trouble hasn't yet lived long enough.

o One must first break before he can be put back together.

o Balance rest on the extremes of adversity and the abundance of prosperity.

o Troubles are problems in which God sends his blessings.

o The best help that a man can receive at times is not to receive any help.

o Blessings from God are hidden in man's problems; it is up for man to search them out.

o Power to go forward often comes from having first gone backwards.

o A loss always spurs the memory.

o The person not carrying a burden is being a burden.

o God's goodness is not to be measured upon one's happiness.

o There are just as many reasons to be found to have a good day than there are to have a bad day.

o Time served is a life lived.

o When everything is bad, God is still good.

o Every clear sky will be visited by bad weather, so will the good man by dark times.

o The pains of loss never leave but its view gradually fades.

o Progress moves man pass one problem only to arrive at yet another.

o The only way to avoid dying is by not being born.

o Failure creeps into one's hand as success slips out of his reach.

o Without the valley there are no hills.

o As the times get darker opportunities to shine become brighter.

o The best possibility of a win is often found when there's nothing left to lose.

o The best chance for success is often found in the worst probability of defeat.

o The greatest pains from the sins of a true follower of Christ are not the effects of them, but rather the knowledge of having committed them.

o Everything that is good for you is not good to you.

o What spanking is for the child; chastening is for the adult.

o Without correction everything would be wrong.

o The man who doesn't struggle with his sins is merely a man who is no longer fighting his sins.

o Life's greatest blessings often come through our worst trials.

o The cold of winter is as certain as the warmth of summer.

o The abuse of medicine is too often more dangerous than illness it treats.

o A costly end often stems from a worthless start.

o A climb begins with a step, yet a slip ends with a fall.

o The man who doesn't take a position will be loved, while the man who does will be hated.

o Nothing delights the devil more than to see man miserable.

o A life must first be broken in order to be put back together.

o Some lives are spared so that others can be saved.

o No marker is more permanent than death.

o Strength always follows the suffering of a Christian.

o Character is generated through difficulty.

#26

Temptation (Detest)

There hath no temptation taken you but such as is common to man: but God [is] faithful, who will not suffer you to be tempted above that ye are able; but will with the temptation also make a way to escape, that ye may be able to bear [it].

1st Corinthians 10:13 KJV

o When you start flirting with an uncertain relationship, you're in danger of wrecking the sure one you have.

o Some accept attention, some demand attention, some refuse attention, but all are visited by attention.

o Satan uses prosperity and fear to fuel a man's motives for this life. God uses prosperity and fear to fuel a man's motives for the next life.

o Want verses need is man's greatest struggle.

o As the mouse is drawn by the cheese so is man trapped by that which he is starved.

o The one who tires of fighting sin will find strength to make excuses for it.

o Those who believe in righteousness will be hated by those who oppose it.

o If the right eye doesn't get you the left one will.

o The greatest battle that you will ever broadly contend with will be wagged within the small confines of your mind.

o What a man is given to, he will be taken by.

o Man is to enjoy many things in this life but love nothing of this world.

o Everything appeals to man more the further that he is off from it.

o The heat of the moment will intrigue you, but the reality of the next will burn you.

o Wants destroys will.

o The fallen can bounce back, but few rarely as high.

o A thought can ruin a man, but a man who thinks can be delivered.

o A many of graves have been dug by a few teeth.

o The flames of the forbidden always leave one with ashes.

o Association might not make you do; however, it can change your desire to do.

o Though wickedness is sweet to the flesh it's bitter to the soul.

o Following every test is a temptation.

o One drive that every man will begin but will never end is his sexual drive.

o You cannot mingle without mixing.

o There's a vast difference in entertaining a thought and going through with the idea.

o The best way to keep from going down the wrong path is to look another direction.

o A moment's pleasure often causes a lifetime of grief.

o Don't risk what you cannot afford to lose.

o Nothing tastes good to the one that is full.

o A moment's decision can yield a lifetime resolution.

o Beware of the seller who doesn't own stock in the company himself.

o Opportunities are to be investigated before initiated.

o Desire never quits on the man; he quits on desire.

o Temptation says I can, commitment says I won't.

o The attraction of the flame is unavoidable, but the union there with is unbearable.

o We're all tempted but not all persuaded.

o With each single temptation there are always multiple choices.

- The man who forgets why he left will remember his path and return.
- A lifetime of hard work can be dispelled by a moment of poor decision.
- The one trip that every man will take and that no man can stop is his sexual drive. The drive is healthy and pleasant, so long as it takes you to the right location.
- What comes naturally is to be controlled not abused.
- Addiction is the decision to be undisciplined.
- Discipline cures what addiction plagues.
- If you give the devil an inch, he will take a foot. And if he takes a foot, he will leave you crippled.
- Influence produces outcome.
- Opening the door for entry closes another means of escape.
- The man that toys with the gun shoots his own self.
- Just because a man is not stepping out into sin doesn't mean that he is not leaving room for it to come in.
- The only way to keep the devil out is to never make any room for him to come in.
- Temptation promotes decision.
- Just as the lure is to the fish so is the flesh to all of mankind.
- If Satan can get you to give a little, he will end up taking a lot.
- The man who lingers around the lose woman will end up holding her parts.
- What a dog's bark threatens the cat's meow subdues.

o   Where God is left out, Satan is brought in.

#27

Thankfulness
(Ingratitude)

Praise ye the LORD. O give thanks unto the LORD; for [he is] good: for his mercy [endureth] for ever.

Psalms 106:1 KJV

o Being of a valiant personality is the best thing since sliced bread to others when they are hungry; but when they are full, audaciousness is impossible to be swallowed.

o It is better to have barely hit it than to have completely missed it.

o Don't merely highlight the cost, underline the benefits.

o Little is more believable than to see many so miserable of those being successful on their very own behalf.

o When you're having a Monday, so is everyone else.

o Don't get lost in all your troubles; find the goodness in that which God has blessed you.

o Chasing the dog that doesn't want to be caught will only end you up having been bitten.

o Enjoy today, it will never be again.

o When you're employed at a grocer you don't buy your bread somewhere else.

o Often the tired man desires to be injured, and the injured man desires to be tired.

o Strength for today, it's a powerful thing.

o Wisdom is the jewel that cannot be given it must be sought for, extracted by, and stored with only those who are desirous of its beauty.

o If you have your health, it doesn't matter how old you are: If you don't have your health, it doesn't matter how old you are.

o Good health is better to be appreciated than bad conditions are to be exclaimed.

o It's not so much to know what you have eaten but to know that you have eaten.

o An apology should always be as big as the offense.

o Value greatly your every day, for its temporal treasure will be forever gone tomorrow.

o The poor man never provided employment for those in need of work, but the rich man has prevented much poverty.

o Boredom also suggests a lack of troubles.

o Never seek to find sympathy but always demand that understanding be found readily available.

o Appreciation for good health is most understood when it is no longer.

o The complainer cannot be silenced but those that praise will prevail.

o There are just as many reasons to be found to have a good day than there are to have a bad day.

o The only satisfaction found is in being satisfied.

o To be rich is to be content.

o It's not to have everything you want, but to appreciate everything you have.

o It's good to have everything you want, it's better to be in good standings with God with what you got.

o Man's expression of thanks is often voiced in his abstinence of ridicule.

o You can't miss what you never had.

o Only the man that is gone can be missed.

o You can only repeat a first but never recapture it.

#28

Trust (Hesitancy)

In all thy ways acknowledge him, and he shall direct thy paths.

Proverbs 3:6 KJV

o Man is only shown what someone else has decided for him to see.

o One should not follow sincerity, for sincerity is often used as a mask by the insincere. Instead pursue truth, truth will never mislead you.

o One should not follow sincerity, for sincerity is often used as a mask by the insincere. Instead pursue truth, truth will never mislead you.

o Don't allow someone else to tell you who he is, let truth tell you himself.

o Those who have interest in the machine will have avoidance in the truth.

o A true answer is more often found where there is absolutely no question any longer to be sought.

o Not everyone wants to hear your prayer request; some just want to know your business.

o Never accept silence as ingratitude or praise as admiration; Faithfulness reveals much.

o Those who refuse that which is biblical will too often be seen acting more spiritual.

o The one, whom can tap into your emotions, can take control of your actions.

o You can't have an honest conversation with the dishonest.

o If one will call you out in public, imagine what they have been doing to you in private.

o When one proves themselves undependable, it should be depended upon.

o The greatest tragedy in life is often found in entrusting someone else with it.

o The most important chapter is the last one, for it can change the entire perception of the book.

o The sinless has either been deceived or is seeking to deceive.

o Love holds no grudge, but it is the foolish that retains a short memory.

o The flatterer will applaud one in their weaknesses, but the truthful will direct them to their strengths.

o An experience is a start, not a conclusion.

o The follower desires to help, the stalker only seeks to harm.

o The deceitful relies on distraction, but clarity is always the path of the honest.

o The magician is skillful, but not truthful.

o Proclaiming a truth deceptively is lying.

o A lie is the outcome, but not the motivation; Sin is often hidden behind a truth, and the deceitful will use this deception and will use it well.

o It's not about the main thing but the other things; for it is the other things that lead to the main thing.

o An effect comes from a big thing; an affect comes from the small things.

o Preference is not truth, and necessity is not a lie; both however are often bearded.

o The magician will have you follow his hand, but the legitimate will reveal the truth.

o Trying to grab the slick tends to be challenging, but the evidence they were there can always be found between the fingers.

o Liberalism: People get it, but they choose not to see it; they are only spiritually blind.

o People will flatter you today and smatter you tomorrow; seek to please the only one that matters.

o Job's friend heard from a Spirit and condemned him.

o One can spend his life pouring into a basket that can't be filled; Look for holes.

o Three type of people: Those that will make a mistake, those that will make a move, and those that will only make a mess.

o Those who ask for your opinion often seek to only discover your position.

o The un-repentant are going to do what they want to do and then try and wrap them all up in grace. The repentant will wrap themselves all up in truth so to strive not to do all that they would want.

o For some, confusion is real; but clarification is always found in the King-James Version bible.

o Hope with you heart but think with your head.

o Truth not welcomed is viewed as a threat, and the threatened will be seen denying the truth.

o As things tighten up you recognize what's lose.

o Having a leader who will say something and have others to believe him is a wonderful thing.

o There is no art more colorful than the pivot.

o Over spicing is as distasteful as watering it down.

o It's not that thirty-days don't count, but thirty-years add up.

o When you don't know what someone is capable, they can surprise you; when you do know what they are capable of you shouldn't be surprised.

o Compliments and flattery bare a close resemblance but smell completely different.

o If you forget what someone is capable of, they will remind you.

o The question is not what one says about his religion, but what that religion says about the man.

o Man cannot bargain with and or reason with evil, he can only be deceived by it.

o Proof has no need for promises, but promises to have no need for proof.

o If one is not a part of the faith, then he is not con-nected to it.

o Evil often masks itself just left of the right.

o One can give truth without giving love, but he can't give love without truth.

o Liberals excel in one area of wisdom unlike that of conservatives; they have the unique ability to show one how not to use it.

o Everybody needs a break, some need fixing.

o Loyalty and consistency rise above flair and gener-osity or should.

o Everyone deserves a measure of love and respect, but not all should be given our kiss and smooch.

o Those being nice can be deceitful, but the heart of kindness will always treat you in turn.

o The aroma of pleasantness is a sweet savor, but the scent of deceit will ruin any appetite.

o A man's hands will unveil what his mouth seeks to hide.

o There is no mistake where a pattern of bad behavior has been established.

o The man who sees himself as the victim will likely be seen by few as the hero.

o A crisis unites or divides, unveils or hides those who are real from those that live a life of lies.

o Most care to hear little from few until they have accomplished much.

o Wisdom can be seen in words, but it is more often heard by sight.

o We are to be thankful for every profession but can only be hopeful for each individual possession.

o No tongue sounds better to the ear than that of praise; but it the mouth of rebuke should be equally sought.

o Age accelerates accuracy.

o While the good man seeks to be at peace, the evil man will find another means to war.

o There can be no treaty of peace with those who are given to break it.

o Loyalty cannot be seen in the beginning but can be proved in the end.

o There is no wrong in seeking to be beautiful, but only ugliness can be found in the heart of a seducer.

o The one that must second guess it, tends to merely seek to deny it.

o The man who desires to be viewed as decent and respectful will seek to dress decent and respectful.

o When you're unsure of God's voice check with his written word.

o What isn't touched cannot be held.

o Everyone talks in confidence when they're in private.

o It is in the multiplication of words that doesn't add up.

o The truth isn't necessarily a complaint, but a lie is always a deceiver.

o One can make a many of difference.

o Be careful of the man not willing to show his position, for that man hasn't likely established one.

o Consider all interpretations but demand the same script.

o Protection never begins with disarmament.

o When one truly believes in Christ Jesus others won't have as hard a time believing in him.

o From the surface, politics and justice resemble each other, seeking, establishing and dispersing favor. However, the core of both can be quite the opposite.

o That which one is most consumed by will he be dispersed with.

o It is better to be in a vehicle with a careful skeptic than a reckless believer.

o The one who sides with God may never measure up but will certainly never disagree.

o Entertaining the words from the foolish may bring a little excitement, but its grand claims are merely just for show.

o Council that man takes in is reflected in the way he outwardly lives.

o Gift givers can be deceiving, but the way of Christ will always be the truth.

o The way to get someone to trust you in the future is to have them experienced belief in you in the past.

o The strongest lock that man will ever find to secure his goods can be opened by a simple key.

o Response always reveals position to the trained eye.

o A tiger that has been removed of his teeth cannot bite, neither can a man destroy that which God has ordained.

o If man will take care of his today, God will take care of his tomorrow.

o Being on the right path may not reveal exactly where one is going, but that man will find comfort in knowing that he will end up exactly where he is supposed to be.

o Once a truth has been altered it is no longer reliable.

o Consider all interpretations but demand the same script.

o The spirit of a man often sees and hears more, and yet is trusted the least.

o A secret enemy will flatter you, but an obvious friend will enlighten you.

o The one who isn't convinced will have a hard time, convincing others.

o Man shouldn't be listening to the message of one's color but rather the color of one's message.

o By listening to the Spirit, you can hear what is not being said.

o Truth isn't always popular and rarely is the popular always truthful.

o Favor fuels power.

o Borrowing is wrong only when you know that you cannot pay it back.

o Much is to be said about faithfulness, little must be said about unfaithfulness.

o The threat of an iceberg always lays hidden just below the slick surface, as does the possible harm behind every smooth smile.

o A lost testimony is hard to recover.

o Proof only ensures what has happened.

o The doctor that condones sin is sick.

o The only surprises in life should be if you never receive any surprises.

o Whenever one comes to the place that they can no longer talk with you they will have begun to talk about you.

o Whenever one begins to talk about you, they will have begun to work against you.

o What can no longer be hidden will often then be distortedly displayed.

o Being polished shouldn't be mistaken for being clean.

o A little persuasion arrests the greatest resistance.

o Emotion displayed out of order cause's commotion.

o A vehicle left in neutral can easily be moved in either direction. So can a man's opinion who hasn't determined any standard.

o The man not trying to be the answer is often insisting on being the problem.

- o A good name laid in ruin is harder to be raised than democracy among socialist.
- o Those not trying to be an answer are only contributing to the problem.
- o People that only move, don't change.
- o The only people that you can be certain of that won't turn their back on you are the ones six foot under looking up at you.
- o Priorities are lived not breathed.
- o If Christ is first in a man's life everything else will be second.
- o A firearm should be as standard as a first-aid kit, fire extinguisher and a spare tire.
- o Anything being poured on too heavy is trying to cover something else up.
- o Can't is the closest word possible used to camouflage the word ain't.
- o Flipping the pillow provides freshness without change; so does a new expression provide renewal for the same truth.
- o The measure of a man's relationship can be determined by his devotion.
- o A little doubt can damage a lot of truth.
- o Influence in mightier than strength.
- o No government can do any greater damage to a nation than can its deceiving ministers.
- o Putting politics above principal is below debate.
- o A lack of dedication prompts the question of qualification.
- o A silent uproar is a false peace.

o Faithfulness counts while disloyalty subtracts.

o It's ok to extend confidence in everyone, just so long as the outcome has already been confirmed.

o Acceptance merely promotes one's view but does not affirm its accuracy.

o Legacy must be built, maintained and preserved.

o Plowing with someone else heifer does not inspire confidence in the farmer.

o It's more likely to have someone look up to you when you haven't let them down.

o Never put but so much trust into anyone, including yourself; if you do, both will surprise you.

o Anyone is capable of anything at any time.

o Know those who do not labor among you.

o People can be governed, but only as far as they will allow you.

o Time and harvest always reveal the seed sewn.

o With greater admiration comes greater responsibility.

o Integrity yields honesty.

o Respect demands responsibility.

o The easiest way to deceive is to counterfeit.

o It's not an enemy that hurts you the most; it's more often a friend.

o You can often tell when you've touched a sore spot by the pain you then receive.

o True nervousness does not come from preparation but the lack thereof.

o The maneuvers of politics are much like the exercises of war; they most often lead to detonation.

- o The one that could eat you up is generally the one that will bite you.
- o The one who doesn't take a side is often given a pass. The one who takes the pass is often given a take.
- o It's easier to destroy a strong city than to build back up a torn down name.
- o It's easier to destroy strength than to revive weakness.
- o The man who is easily persuaded is rarely pursued.
- o The most valuable possession man can own is this life his reputation.
- o The follower depends on his leader.
- o The one doing better has been worse.
- o Being much improved means, one has been very bad.
- o To Fear is not to sin, to yield to God's will because of that fear is.
- o Every promise comes with a condition.
- o Promises of the bible are quoted by many but their conditions are spoken by few.
- o A proverb being voiced from the mouth of a fool is like water being offered from the spillage of raw sewage.
- o No picture can be more cunning or deceitful than the smile.
- o Influence is the most powerful asset a man has.
- o By not answering the question being posed, it yields more questions about the poise of the one being asked.
- o A dog without teeth cannot bite; neither can the man whose word is in ruin.
- o The man that is politically correct is spiritually wrong.

o To go right is to say that there is one way, to go left is to say that there are other ways.

o The inside of a thing is never the same as the outside of a thing.

o Motive should be evaluated above every action that is appreciated.

o If you're not straight, you're crooked.

o The discerning eye can see through the blurred lips and into the clear heart.

o Fear is merely an illusion used to prompt or prevent advancement.

o Fear produces anticipation for the bad, while God's word produces anticipation for the good.

o The reason why you don't hear of one's position is because they don't want you to know their position.

o Personality doesn't define character, but acts of kindness are often used to hide a lack of it.

#29

Truth (Lies)

Lying lips [are] abomination to the LORD:
but they that deal truly [are] his delight.

Proverbs 12:22 KJV

o One should not strive to be sincere, for one can be sincere yet be sincerely wrong. Instead, one should strive to be right.

o Nothing in history is more important than the future.

o If man's life isn't being filtered by truth, he is living a lie.

o Say it softly if you can, express it loudly if you must.

o To hide behind a truth is to deceive another with a false.

o Telling a truth wrongfully is as sinful as telling a lie truthfully.

o Right will always be right no matter how wrong man tries to make it.

o One either conforms to the truth or is condemned by it.

o Wherever there has been a circus someone has to come along behind with a shovel and clean it up.

o A deceptive insinuation is as sinful as a false accusation.

o One should discover the truth and take its position, not take a position and look for a truth.

o Making twisted trendy doesn't straighten, and unpopularizing that which is right won't wrong.

o Where false narratives are claimed, solid truths are made to question.

o The uncivil may threaten the respectful to be quiet, but the absolute truth will embolden him.

o Choosing not to wear your glasses doesn't remove what is in front of you.

o Don't dilute it nor pollute it, for God's word is the devil's only fear.

o One may not buy the truth, nor sell the truth, but he sure won't change the truth.

o To anyone who wants it, you can get a 50% discount on half a truth.

o Stereotypes could easily be resolved by proving them wrong, plain and simple.

o Where wisdom is absent and knowledge is unavailable, truth is always present.

o The truth should be purchased above all and sold for nothing.

o Dehydration fuels the mirage, and its pursuit will never quench one's thirst.

o Strides to perfection should always be made, but advancement will never come in reverse.

o Truth has no preference, but every false will find an audience.

o That which isn't true can only be erected for a while, but that which isn't false will stand forever.

o Coming to yourself, will be the most important journey one will ever take.

o One can run from the truth, but he will never escape it.

o Truth may age but it never grows old.

o When it all comes down to the truth, the truth is above it all.

o As the shadow confirms a presence, so does the bible affirm the light.

o Where truth cannot be changed its definition will be twisted.

o If there's no difference being reflected in one's life, then there's likely little change that has been erected in one's life.

o Deep thoughts can be overwhelming, but shallow waters won't drown you.

o Left or right, up or down, it all comes down to either right or wrong.

o The truth isn't always popular but it's always the truth.

o Truth should have the last say in any and everything that man questions.

o Anyone can mess up, but the truly repentant will straighten up.

o One will either hate truth or love it. What determines man's position is his motivation.

o Nothing angers the rebellious more than the truth.

o The truth is appreciated only by those who accept it.

o Fact is to be considered above every tact that is delivered.

o Performers may change, but the song remains the same.

o Where truth has been rejected division is certain to be adopted.

o The pains of the truth heal, while the comforts of a lie rot.

o Viewing the left always reassures the right.

o An old saying isn't necessarily a truth, but a truth is always a faithful saying.

o Truth cannot be segregated to cure social ills; it must be administered and that without prejudice.

o Without truth there can be no restrictions.

o Excuses cannot provide answers.

o Proclaiming the truth doesn't confirm its practice; neither does practice deny its existence.

o Liberalism is the escape from the truth; Conservatism is the pursuit of it.

o If the labeling of the ingredients is accurate, its content cannot be denied.

o Truth may cause pain today, but denial is certain to continue the hurt tomorrow.

o Putting the King-James version bible into a church helps get the hell out of it.

o If one believes what God's word says to be the truth, how much more then should the truth be protected by one's belief?

o People don't generally change that much, you just get to know them a little better.

o A moral conscious can be severed, but the truth cannot be changed.

o No complex lie is more painful than the plain truth.

o One's standing depends upon firm ground.

o A lack of understanding doesn't deny the definition.

o To tell a lie to escape a trouble is foolish; to tell a misguided truth to cause a trouble is fool.

o Statistics, although revealing, are only as good as the accuracy of their reporting.

o Statistics illuminate that which has been left in the dark.

o Opinions can be rejected, but the truths can't be denied.

o A true answer is more often found where there is absolutely no question any longer to be sought.

o Evidence only points towards the truth, but the truth has no need of evidence.

o Truth invested yields long term successes.

o To love the truth is to hate a false.

o Science becomes fiction when its facts become unbiblical.

o An announcement doesn't secure the engagement, neither does denial refuse it.

o A truth spoken untimely is like an accurate watch in the wrong time zone.

o A truth spoken out of season can be wrong.

o Where questions have been ruled out answers will be brought in.

o The truth dis-spirits the boldest and empowers the cowardly.

o Party affiliation should change according to biblical application.

o There can be only one truth, yet many lies.

o Trapped in a rut or to be all over the road; both are challenging.

o A good truth misapplied is a bad lie.

o No response to nonsense says more than many words.

o Entertainment delays misery, Enlightenment avoids it.

o Understanding can be made clear, but truth can only be muddied up.

o Where there is no central truth there will be many fallacies.

o An interpretation is not to be argued but a truth is to be exclaimed.

o Where there are two truths there is one lie.

o Truth separates a many of friend, but deception brings together the fool.

o Where the presence of more than one truth is so is the assurance of a lie.

o Deceit goes easy and the truth comes hard.

o The truth does not hate, a lie does.

o You can't have a perversion without first having a truth.

o You cannot have a false without a truth, but you can have a truth without a false.

o Versions of right may be wrong, but right cannot be wronged by versions.

o The minister that can no longer preach the truth needs repentance, revival and or relocation.

o The parishioners that can no longer tolerate truth needs repentance, revival and or relocation.

o The foolish will tell a lie to attempt to get out of a trouble, while the fool will tell a lie to begin a trouble.

o Truth can be delayed but it cannot be stopped.

o Truth can stir up anger but racist stir up hate.

o Labeling is often used as a means of warning and not intended to merely reflect a factual statement.

o A Proverb should be used to reflect and accept a fact and not a fault.

o Anything left of center is not right.

o The biggest reductions often come by the smallest additions.

o By adding water, the contents become diluted. So does the continual revisions of God's word.

o Enemies can change, friends can change, but the word of God will remain the same.

o Truth doesn't change, though people change the truth.

o Shades can darken an image, but they cannot change the image.

o Better it is to be recorded than remembered.

o You can never repeat a first.

o Position reveals one's stand.

o Quotes can be confusing, definitions shouldn't.

o When the heart is right the feet will follow it.

o To have itching ears for the un-truth, is to have cursing mouths for the certain truth.

o The guilty will either regret what he has done, or either he will regret that he got caught for it. Wisdom questions, answers, reveal, assigns, and conclude the truth, or lack thereof, of them both.

o The one who cannot finish a sentence without using religious phraseology is one trying to sell something that they likely haven't got.

o You are either living for the devil or dying for Christ.

o The truth can be changed, but you cannot change the truth.

o There may be many interpretations, but there is only one truth.

o   The varying of views on God's Word is to be considered, but the changing of God's Word is not.

o   The bible is open for interpretation, but the word of God is closed on change.

o   A Proverb is inclusive but not exclusive.

o   What type of mother will not force medicine on her child if it will make them better? So it is with a friend that won't speak the truth to his brother.

o   An enemy will cover deceit with a smile; a friend will uncover truths with compassion.

o   Addition or Subtraction can multiply division.

o   The meaning of God's word should be exercised, while the changing of God's word should be demonized.

o   Truth never lies.

o   To deter one from the truth is to lead one to a lie.

o   One must realize where he is at before he can get to where he's going.

o   The circle says that there is no need for a beginning or an end.

o   Any truth contrary to God's word is a lie.

o   By politically categorizing one side as the right defines the left to be exactly what it is.

o   Getting to the point causes a sting.

o   Being direct seeks to expose truth, while meandering only seeks to flatter the foolish.

o   The man who has many excuses escapes few indictments.

o   The man who is full of excuses will be void of answers.

o   The bible cuts or soothes according to its application.

o Prophecy may be prevented but history cannot be erased.

o Volume is often elevated to lower the voice of the educated.

o Interpretation is always open; the truth is always closed.

o The preacher that never corrects a mistake fails his congregation.

o Not every man shall sleep, but every man shall be awakened.

#30

Tongue (Keep Quiet)

Whoso keepeth his mouth and his tongue
keepeth his soul from troubles.

Proverbs 21:23 KJV

o When you give your two cents, be prepared for someone else to hand you the other ninety-eight.

o Not everyone is making a prayer request; some are just sharing the news.

o The one, who slings the dirt, is often unknowingly, digging their own grave.

o It's impossible to sound bad keeping quiet.

o For most, it isn't the teeth that bite, but rather the tongue. Guard it well.

o Heavenly language should be accompanied with godly living.

o The condition of the heart should be more significant than the expression of the tongue.

o The loudest voice is often the one that isn't being heard.

o The tongue has no teeth, yet it can bite you.

o It is a terrible thing to not know what to say, it is worse to say a thing and not know how to say it.

o Being direct and to the point leaves little doubt and is never dull.

o Within' the power of the tongue is the gift to capture or release.

o The heart hides man's deepest deceits, but it is the shallow tongue that easily reveals it.

o The delivery is more readily acceptable than the package.

o If you want more to be heard, say less.

o What one barks about the loudest often bites him the hardest.

- To digest the truth, one will have swallowed a mouthful.
- The less you say, the less you pay.
- Freedom of speech comes at a price.
- A woman is only as much of a lady as is her language.
- The delivery is more effective than the pitch.
- Words can both sweeten and bitter.
- The man that shows his position is destined to have opposition.
- Conservative values are not supported by a liberal vocabulary.
- Where there is nothing good to be said little should be heard.
- The man who seeks to hide another man's fault seeks to secure his love, but the one who strives to always uncover it will lose it.
- The only way to keep something from getting around is not to ever pass it out.
- With the right of freedom of speech should also come the expectation of penalty.
- Words of the wise are those that are often left unsaid.
- Being blunt causes others to sharpen.
- While a snatch at the wheel can steer you into another direction, it can also quickly put you in the ditch.
- Attention is most often held not by what one says but in how he says it.
- To complain about others complaining is a complaint.
- The person causing noise always becomes a target.

- The greater wrath is kindled through another's truth not their lie.
- The one who shares many secrets will have few contributors.
- There is more to be seen in one's speech than can be heard from one's voice.
- The exposed tongue reveals the hidden heart.
- Favor is found in favorable speech.
- Well-chosen words prevent bad selected responses.
- Man's greatest help and or his greatest hurt will come from what he says.
- The tongue is merely an outlet from the source.
- More fires have been started by the tongue than all the matches that has ever been lit.
- The heart of the wise quickens the ignorance of his mouth.
- Man's sharpest tool is his tongue.
- The complainer seeks gain but inherits loss.
- Vulgarity loses its shock by regularity.
- Explaining intent to those who are intent not to hear you is impossible.
- As sure as the human eye will blink, so will the tongue fail its owner.
- One sure way to avoid hearing is not to stand around and listen.
- With correction, comes another temptation to wrong.
- Sparing words prolongs friendships.
- The childless always has the answers on parenting; the parent often hasn't a clue.

o The man that says much hides little.

o The one who merely reports the trouble often becomes branded as the trouble.

o The truth should never be apologized, although its delivery should be considered.

o People who can't take advice will always insist on giving it.

o It's not the volume coming from the speaker, but rather who it is making the noise that should be most considered.

o Man is unmasked by what he does, not by what he says.

o The distinguished characteristic of a man that helps him the most, will most often hurt him the most.

o The voice that is never heard is the voice that never speaks.

o Power without a receptacle is of no use; so is the pastor without discretion.

o Too much can be said without finishing what one has to say.

o The one making the loudest noise is noticed more when he is silenced.

o The one who doesn't speak up is hard to be heard.

o When one's question is not quickly answered he may wish to defer the response.

o The complainer is the sister to the backbiter.

o A proverb can convict, condemn, prevent and or free.

o A proverb is a short-based saying of wisdom, truth and morals learned from experience.

o Though a true proverb will stand the test of time, it is important to remember the setting in which it was written.

o The understanding of a proverb can sometimes be taken as a literal meaning in one situation and a different expressive meaning in another.

o The proverb is a phrase that doesn't always follow the normal rules of meaning and or grammar but can institute more knowledge than a college degree.

o A proverb is a bit of practical advice that should be viewed as the rule and not the exception.

o To know a proverb is to know a basic truth about life in an incisive manner.

o There is no escape from criticism or praise neither in life nor in death.

o The man with the loud voice is noticed more in his silence.

o Only the tongue is more deceptive than the smile.

o Be slow to answer a man with a yes and slower to respond to a woman with a no.

o One making a complaint is viewed as a complainer by those who wish not to address it.

o The man that desires to be heard cannot be silenced.

o An expression of gratitude delivers a bounty of satisfaction.

o The one that measures his words guards his ruler.

o Controversy fuels conversation.

o Much is heard where little is said.

o The man that refuses to reap contentment will continually choose to sow discord.

o When someone steps in it, everyone around them will know it.

#31

Work (Slothfulness)

And whatsoever ye do, do [it] heartily, as to the Lord, and not unto men;

Colossians 3:23 KJV

o Three kinds of people; those who will let you do for them, those that demand you do for them and those who won't let you do for them.

o Two kinds of people: Those who do little and make themselves appear hard at it, and those who are hard at it and make themselves appear at ease.

o Work doesn't ensure riches, but slumber will guarantee want.

o Conservatism doesn't promise you success, but it guarantees that you won't fail. Liberalism promises you will succeed, but it doesn't guarantee that you won't fail.

o If you work, you will hate laziness; If you're lazy you'll love those that work.

o Weeping may endure all night, but 4:00am is still going to come in the morning.

o Three types of workers: One that stirs up the dust, one that stirs dust up the most, and one that simply waits for the dust to settle.

o Success is not crowned, rather it is achieved.

o An education will open many doors, not working will close them.

o The trail of want follows in the path of slumber.

o Work accompanied with faith will leave many miracles.

o Handouts are easily accepted where advice on avoiding its need is readily rejected.

o Welfare too often takes away what people need the most; the incentive to work.

o Ensuring insuring the uninsured only assures the un-insuring of the insured.

o The incentive to get off the wagon will only come in making the ride more uncomfortable.

o When welfare pays more to sit at home than get up to work, the house will have little incentive to leave.

o Where work is the answer, slothfulness is the cause.

o A vision without work is merely a daydream.

o Keeping things together is a job, and where there is no work there can be no expected entitlements.

o Struggle is demanded before any suggested relief.

o One of the best ways to feel good is to tire you out.

o The slothful would rather not work and collect than to have to collect by work.

o Work is the surest cure to all poverty.

o Being a contributor may tire you but being at ease will undoubtedly fire you.

o The best means to improving poverty is education, the only cure is work.

o There is no shame to be seen in doing general labor, although labor is often shamed by the lack of effort being generally seen.

o What is working stops when one stops the working.

o Jobs increase by rewarding the employer, not penalizing him.

o The best way to decrease unemployment is to stop rewarding people for not working.

o A way out provides far more than a bail out.

o Being at ease causes tightness.

o Living in the past will kill your future.

o The harder a man will work the luckier he will become.

o The abuse of entitlements aids expectancy.

o The abundance of entitlements reduces responsibilities.

o Work is the quickest turnaround from poverty to abundance.

o Luck is an unfaithful friend, but work will never desert you.

o Where there is no energy there can be no power.

o Unrest is rarely attributed to over exertion.

o The household that will upkeep for those that reside will need not prepare for those who might would visit.

o Man's nature often reveals his forecast.

o Employment is dependent on work.

o One cannot elevate himself by digging out but rather by climbing up.

o Delay not only postpones the eventual payment, but it generally cost more.

o Seed of any kind is of no use until it has been sewn.

o If one desires to reap the benefits, he should be willing to pay the cost.

o Success should not be expected where work is doubted.

o There is no better economic plan than work.

o You can't give until you first get.

o Grass covers the garden not tilled and poverty the man that won't work.

o Man is helped more when he is helped less.

o Ruin is the cost often priced by abused welfare.

o Helping hurts where ability is deferred.

o Time has no prevalence in eternity.

o You cannot draw water from a dry well.

o Opportunity should come from man's sacrifice not from the sacrificing of man.

o Getting around trouble always calls for more steps.

o Without work there can be no rest.

o The person who does not give their best at what they are doing will likely not give their best with anything else.

o Responsibility reveals reputation.

o Vacancy houses trouble but occupancy has no room for it.

o Although greatness sometimes instantly appears, it is rarely instantaneously born.

o Failure and destruction start small but ends big.

o Failure isn't going to announce its arrival, but rather silently slip in.

o It's good to be a help before you become a need.

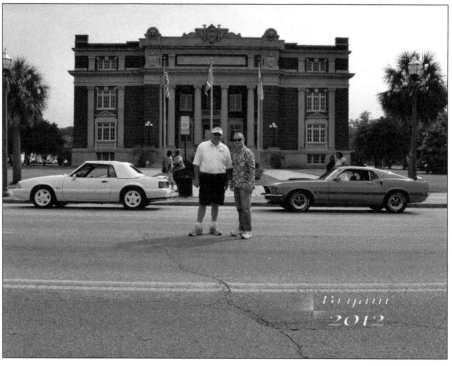

CPSIA information can be obtained
at www.ICGtesting.com
Printed in the USA
LVHW011658291220
675234LV00025B/1055/J

9 781662 801655